THE PERFECT LAWYER

Simon McCrum

BENNION
KEARNY

Published in 2025 by Bennion Kearny Limited

Woodside, Oakamoor, ST10 3AE, UK

www.BennionKearny.com

ISBN: 978-1-915855-40-4

Bennion Kearny Limited. 6 Woodside, Churnet View Road, Oakamoor, ST10 3AE, United Kingdom.

I dedicate this book to my Mum and Dad for their love,
and for their unfailing belief in me.

Books in this Series

Contents

INTRODUCTION

I wrote my first book *The Perfect Legal Business* because I was determined to share with existing, growing, new, and future law firms, and law firm owners, all the lessons I had learned in a career of law firm management and leadership. A career that was peppered with highs and lows, successes and failures.

I wanted to help law firms harness the many things I had done right and to help them avoid the many things I had done wrong.

I had absolutely no expectation that that book would get the reception that it did. Thousands of copies were sold and despatched across some 50 countries.

To watch, for example, a discussion about my book taking place online between lawyers in Africa filled me with pride. As did learning that many leading and already successful UK law firms were basing their whole Partners' Retreats and their new three-year and five-year strategies around my book. As did many small and large law firms buying a copy of the book for each and every one of their people – not just their lawyers.

What really blew me away, though, was the torrent of incredible, completely unsolicited feedback I got from literally hundreds of lawyers and law firms that I'd never met, about how the book had changed their working and business lives.

A wide range of firms have worked hard to implement its tools and recommendations. Others have engaged me to get them into "PLB" shape in a rapid and joined-up way. They are all now enjoying the rewards of their courage.

All of that brings me to this book. I started writing it because I couldn't stop thinking that whilst I could see what *a law firm* needed to do, I felt that "a law firm" can't actually do anything. It needs *its lawyers* to do things, and that it was all down to *them*.

I realised whilst writing this book that I was wrong about that. The firm and the lawyers BOTH need to do things.

My realisation has hopefully produced a book that begins with flowery language like "perfect" and "perfection" but which ends with hard facts, hard truths, and concrete suggestions that will be of value to lawyers and law firms, and help them to make the progress they need.

This book, *The Perfect Lawyer,* flows directly from my first book, *The Perfect Legal Business.* They go together, like hand in glove. Indeed, much more than I realised, as a few things happened while writing this book.

First, the dawning that you can't arrive at *The Perfect Legal Business* unless the lawyers in it all adopt certain "perfect" behaviours.

But second, the dawning that you can't write about The Perfect Lawyer without them being in The Perfect Legal Business! Lawyers can't just start behaving "perfectly" – *they need the firm to adopt various "perfect" behaviours and catalysts, too.*

The end result of these two dawnings is a book that I did not expect to write. I had expected to be writing a free-standing second book. Instead, it is a continuation of the journey for lawyers and law firms that started with my first book. I thought it would be about swashbuckling lawyers. Instead, I can now see clearly that it's all about a collaboration between lawyers and the firm.

I believe that, taken together, the *two* books now are a genuine aid to help lawyers and law firms move in a good direction. But that's only on paper. For I arrived at a third dawning, which I couldn't let go, as I don't like things that only work "on paper". I wanted to go as far as I could to help lawyers and law firms make concrete things happen, on the ground. Therefore, I moved further away from the book I thought I'd be writing.

My third dawning was this: we all already know much of what I write about. There is no rocket science here. We all want to deliver a life-changing service to clients. We all want to make more money. We all want to change the lives of our teams. Lawyers, teams, and firms will say that they've tried most of these things, and they didn't work. Or they didn't work for long.

Therefore, I explore at the end of this book why we don't always achieve these aims in law firms. What gets in the way? How can we remove the obstacles to any change or improvement that a law firm needs?

I write this book as someone who believes that:

- Lawyers can and should change clients' lives

- Many things stop even the most committed lawyers from doing that
- Lawyers and law firms generally aren't generating the maximum business dividend from their expertise and labours
- Many things are stopping that from happening, too
- Change is, therefore, probably needed in many legal businesses
- Change should be a lot easier to achieve than it appears to be
- The obstacles are in the hands of both lawyers and law firms
- The obstacles can all be easily removed

There is no getting away from it. A law firm (by which I mean its owners and Management) can try all it wants to become The Perfect Legal Business, but absent a particular magic ingredient, it will be like pushing a rock up a hill. Any success will ultimately be short-lived or will be absent altogether.

That magic ingredient is a team of lawyers who embrace (and who work as a team to constantly push) a limited set of internal and external priorities and behaviours that – together – will change their clients' lives, the destiny of the legal business they work in, and the lives of themselves and their colleagues.

The lawyers who embrace all the things I talk about in this book can rightly be called The Perfect Lawyer. In being that, they will inevitably create The Perfect Legal Business.

Obviously, in looking here at what makes The Perfect Lawyer from various perspectives, including that of The Perfect Legal Business that employs them, and following on from the "Eureka" moment I had that The Perfect Lawyer doesn't exist in a vacuum and has to be within (and is, in fact, a vital building block of) The Perfect Legal Business, I discuss a number of the areas that were covered in my first book, though perhaps from a different angle.

If my doing so exposes more individual lawyers to the tried and tested business principles that underpin sustainably successful law firms, and helps them as they discharge their role in society, that is no bad thing for clients, for those lawyers, for the law firms they work in, or (forgive me having so grand a thought) for the legal profession as a whole.

In looking at The Perfect Legal Business and The Perfect Lawyers that it needs, I focus here on lawyers who are employed in private practise, and specifically those employed in (what should be) profit-making organisations.

Whilst in-house counsel, or lawyers in the not-for-profit sector, say, may not be engaged in many of the financial rigours that private-practise lawyers are subject to, I hope and believe there will still be much in my books for them. There's far more to being a great lawyer than making maximum money from clients – like changing the lives of your internal and external clients.

So, lawyers, whether you want to be a lawyer or you already are a lawyer, and whatever route you took or are taking, I take my hat off to you. Genuinely.

Anyone who knows me personally or professionally knows how much value and importance I place on the role of lawyers and law firms in society. People turn to us when they need help – often when they are desperately in need of help. We only see people when they bring the biggest and/or most traumatic things in their lives to us.

That is an absolute privilege.

When I was Managing Partner, I used to say to my team, "Anyone who thinks we sell t-shirts should leave now. We don't. We change lives".

I started my Articles (now called the Training Contract) in 1987. After re-sitting all my Final exams (I never did anything the easy way), I eventually qualified as a solicitor in 1990.

In the 30 or so years since then, I have worked incredibly hard, had a riot of fun, made myself very proud on occasions, let myself down badly on other occasions, changed clients' lives, been sued for not changing clients' lives, been given the opportunity to blossom, given other people the opportunity to blossom, been literally in tears with worry and stress, and been literally in tears of joy. Not for one minute have I been bored.

Being a lawyer is hard work. Being a good lawyer is very hard work. Being The Perfect Lawyer can be extremely hard work – but it doesn't have to be like that.

As a lawyer at any level, in what I here call "external" terms, I passionately believe that you can – you *should* –

change your clients' lives rather than just go through the motions or even make clients' lives worse.

As a member of a law firm team, I passionately believe that, in "internal" terms, you can – you *should* – add positively to the life of that community, a community which it can be an overlooked privilege to be a part of. Make the community a great place!

Further, in "internal" terms, as a lawyer in private practise, I also passionately believe you absolutely have to add to the financial performance of *the business* that you are part of, for your own good, for the good of everyone in it, and for the good of everyone it serves.

And, as a senior lawyer who has attained partnership and who leads lawyers or teams or who leads or owns the whole firm, I passionately believe that you can – you *should* – change the lives of everyone around you in that firm.

These external and internal dimensions all add up to a *purpose* that should add fuel to your fire every day.

I often ask lawyers at law firms with whom I work, "Are you a great lawyer?" None has ever replied "No".

But what makes a "great lawyer"? It depends on who you are asking. As I have hinted at already, there are external and internal dimensions to the question.

Let me give you some examples:

- The lawyer who drafts an amazing 15-page legal advice to a client, that the client doesn't understand, and for which the lawyer charges a lot of money – a great lawyer?

- The lawyer who is working hard behind the scenes but whose stressed clients never know where their case is up to – a great lawyer?

- The lawyer who is great at getting clients, who doesn't go home until all calls are returned, who does a good job on the technical law front, who fights like a tiger for clients, but who makes no money for their law firm because they quote low prices, don't record all their time spent on client files, and who discount WIP when it comes to billing – a great lawyer?

- The hard-working lawyer who is the highest biller in the firm, who has a fortune in unbilled disbursements on their Matter Printout and many of whose bills never get paid – a great lawyer?

- The high-billing and "top-ranked-in-Chambers" lawyer, who cannot retain any junior lawyers because they are, well, horrible – a great lawyer?

What makes The Perfect Lawyer, therefore, has to be looked at from a number of perspectives, which can be grouped into external and internal perspectives:

- From the perspective of clients – external

- From the perspective of the business – internal

The individual lawyers in the Perfect Legal Business are fundamentally important when it comes to a law firm ticking all the "PLB" boxes. The "boxes" that directly depend on the input of the individual lawyers include:

- The building of a brand (or promise) that all a firm's lawyers deliver on, all the time, which includes real differentiators that are more than just words on a website

- A high level and quality and proactivity of service – every client, every lawyer, every time

- An exacting (rather than an easy) engagement with clients, where there is "pride in pricing", a defined and limited retainer, and an emphasis on quick payment

- Making maximum fees (and cash) on every case, by a combination of pricing the work correctly, doing the work fully and in a timely way (and not snatching time on the file or even putting the file into storage), recording all the time that is spent, looking out for "mission creep", billing all the time that has been recorded, and ensuring the client pays you quickly

- Looking at the client in a holistic way – as a *client* rather than as a case (and certainly not as *my* client) – and working hard to ensure all clients avail themselves of the services of every team in your firm (cross-caring, as opposed to cross-selling)

- Not waiting for the phone to ring, but rather cross-caring in a proactive way

I look at all of these areas in detail in this book. Together, they add up to a lawyer being deserving of the title The Perfect Lawyer.

I also explore the symbiosis between lawyer and law firm – their interdependency:

- It won't work if the lawyers just demand things from the firm. In the words of JFK – "Ask not what your firm can do for you…"

- And it won't work if the firm just demands things from the lawyers. In the words of JFK – "Ask not what your lawyers can do for you…"

This book could just as well be called "The Perfect Collaboration".

But even when efforts are made to collaborate, whether that be to try old things in new ways, or to try new things altogether, the wheels can all-too-easily come off.

This is a particular risk in law firms. Meetings – what can I say? I have sat in countless meetings in law firms and watched them all too quickly veer off the desired path, or hit bumps, or smash into walls. Things can get talked to death, or they can get crushed to death.

We have to be self-aware here, and – as I do in a number of areas in this book – we have to actually build failure into the plan and have mechanisms for overcoming those obstacles.

First thing's first, though. As I say, on the face of it, the qualities of The Perfect Lawyer can be grouped into external and internal. This book is therefore divided into these two sections, and it is to the first of these that we now turn.

Simon McCrum, 2025

PART 1

FROM THE EXTERNAL PERSPECTIVE – CLIENTS

CHAPTER 1

CLIENTS, AND THE
SERVICE THEY WANT

I have read various surveys over the years that say how lots of clients are unhappy with the service they get from law firms. I have heard lots of stories from people I have talked with directly who say the same.

I have had lots of personal experiences as a client, where the service I have received has been woeful. Only recently, because we hadn't heard anything for a long time, did we chase one firm of lawyers, only to be told by a secretary, "You have to understand, we are inundated with work". Incredible. Shocking. Again.

In identifying "service" as a great opportunity for law firms, I don't rely on any of that, though. Many, many lawyers can point to 5-star reviews they've had from clients.

I rely on something altogether more telling than any public survey could generate. Those surveys could only ever capture feedback from dozens or hundreds of people. And the main people who talk about the service they've received are those with complaints. There could be many more who are happy with the service they've received.

Therefore, I listen to what law firms and lawyers themselves are telling me.

Over the years, I have spoken with many dozens of law firms and many hundreds of lawyers. Between them, they have *many, many thousands* of cases that – they tell me – they are simply not getting around to working on, or working on properly, because they can't.

That adds up to many, many thousands of clients who are waiting to hear about, and to see good progress on, what is probably the biggest thing in their life.

It would be absurd to try to weigh up what makes The Perfect Lawyer without taking into account what "perfect lawyer" means to clients.

Indeed, many lawyers rely *solely* on what clients think of them to demonstrate that they are "perfect".

The client absolutely wants a great service from their lawyer. That is, a great service in *their* terms.

The moment that work begins on a client's case is the acid test for the law firm. Is its service going to be spectacularly 'normal' (which, believe me, can be erratic and awful), or spectacularly good and therefore truly different?

The firm has to do a good job and deliver a great service – every lawyer, every time – if it is to not only keep that case and keep that client but also do what The Perfect Legal Business always does. That is, to see the case not as a *case* but as a *client* and to extend maximum care, including proactively, to that client. Firms often call this cross-selling, but I call it cross-caring, and it is the way to secure a lifetime's value out of every good client, their family, and their business.

If you are able to explain to a client not just what a great service they will get, but also *how it is* that you can make so bold a statement, this can be a real differentiator that gets clients to come to you, and to choose to use you (even if you're dearer than other quotes they've had).

Lots of law firms say they are service-driven. I don't know how they can say that!

Why you should use me / my firm

Here's a challenge to all lawyers reading this. Complete this sentence as if you were sitting in front of a potential client:

"You should use *me* because…"

I can only think of *three* things here that could meaningfully be said by a lawyer in response. The first is hard to claim and substantiate. The second is not something you should go anywhere near. The third, though, is something to aspire to.

"I'm the best"

Words that would be powerful here include, "I'm simply the best in this area of law, and this is all I do. There isn't anything in this area of law that I haven't seen and solved".

For many an individual or family or business with a complex legal situation, engaging the lawyer who is known as "the best" in that field is a "must", whatever the price.

It is up to the lawyer whether they want to charge a premium price as a result of them being "the best".

Being "the best" is a superb differentiator – everyone else is an also-ran.

In this vein, I recall that when I was Managing Partner, we procured a new Practise Management System for my law firm. As part of the process, we were presented with a thick contract by the supplier. I wanted to know what that contract said both in letter and in spirit, so I researched who the best lawyer in the region was for advising on IT contracts.

I contacted him and he explained that he charged £10,000 plus VAT – before he'd even seen the contract. That's a ridiculous price, but from our conversation and my research, it was clear that he was indeed superb at this stuff – and he turned out to be invaluable. The fee paled against the value he added.

That's the power of being known as "the best" – it's a real differentiator. He converted me from an enquiry into a client, and he set the price high! He had the confidence to refuse to budge.

"I'm the cheapest"

Some clients might like to hear this. As someone "in the know", I would run a mile from a firm that said they were the cheapest.

There's no way they could be "the cheapest" and still have great expertise on my case and on the end of a phone for me. To be the cheapest, you'd have to be cutting corners somewhere.

"I'll give you an amazing service – guaranteed"

In response to the above question, the lawyer might say, "You'll always get an amazing service from me. What you'll get is my personal approach to looking after clients. I'll always push your case, and I'll always tell you where things are up to".

Push and tell!

That's really compelling, particularly if the question has come from a client who has had bad service from a lawyer in the past.

So, those are the three answers you might give when a client is talking about using *you*.

Next, can I ask the lawyers reading this to complete the following sentence as if they were sitting in front of a potential client where, this time, the client has a *broad range* of legal needs:

"You should use *my firm* for *all your legal needs* because…"

It's a different challenge now, isn't it?

Is the lawyer really going to reply, "You should use my firm for all your legal needs because *all* my colleagues are *the best* in their fields"?

Or because "All my colleagues are the cheapest in town", too?

Or is the lawyer really going to be able to say, "You should use my firm for all your legal needs because *all* my colleagues will deliver an amazing service all the time"?

The first response, in my view, doesn't hold water and wouldn't be a credible claim.

The second is not a claim you should be making.

The third, though, around "amazing service" from all the lawyers in the firm, would be compelling – if it were true.

However, with the best will in the world, even when talking about just yourself, a lawyer may not always be able to give an amazing service. They might have a huge caseload, with files already on their desk that they can't get around to dealing with. Or they might be tied up on a big case, or they might be ill or on holiday, or have little in the way of support from good, junior lawyers.

Lawyers – even great lawyers – can fall short on both the "push the case" and the "tell the client" fronts through no fault on their part.

A lawyer cannot usually guarantee to a potential new client that even they will themselves always be able to deliver an amazing service, let alone make that boast about all of their colleagues. They, too, might be stuck down at court, or on holiday, or ill, or just be overwhelmed.

So, it's difficult to make that "service" boast on an individual, let alone a collective, level. Which is a real shame, as it's an extremely powerful thing to be able to boast.

To my mind, the ability of a lawyer and a law firm to *genuinely* boast that "We deliver a great service – every lawyer, every time, across the whole firm" is *the* differentiator par excellence.

It is a game-changer in so many ways and is a foundation of The Perfect Legal Business, of The Perfect Lawyer, and therefore of this book.

It is possible. We did it. "A great service – *every* lawyer, *every* time" was our whole strategy when I was Managing Partner. It's what we hung our hat on. And we went public with it in an extreme way. We all knew it, believed in it, and were proud of it. This was – for us – not a hollow boast but rather something that we invested a good deal of time, money, energy, passion, courage, determination, and (now outdated) technology in.

"Service". The very word is more complicated in this forum than you might at first think.

From a client's perspective, "great service" consists of a host of aspects and behaviours on the part of their lawyer:

- Legal technical knowledge – it's not much of a service if the lawyer doesn't know the law

- An ability to frame that technical knowledge into practical, understandable, real-life, sensible options

- An ability to communicate that advice and those options in a way that lay clients will understand

- An acceptance by the lawyer that a client will get more out of you, and you out of them, by you talking rather than just by relying on letters or texts or emails

- The lawyer being accessible and responsive

- The lawyer doing all of this within a reasonable timescale

- The lawyer not running up costs on things that don't progress the case – see the "one unit" issue, later in this book

- Cheaper junior work being done by cheaper junior lawyers

- The lawyer always pushing the case

- The lawyer always telling the client where things are up to

- The lawyer always making the client feel better, not worse. (It's effectively all about "Push & Tell")

If you could "Push & Tell" on a case, every lawyer and every time, you'd avoid the most frequent complaints about law firms' service levels.

You'd also avoid many of the Professional Negligence claims that arise.

And you'd have both *a brand* (that is, a promise) which is an extremely valuable differentiator, and an ever-expanding list of clients (all of whom would join your salesforce).

All too often, though, what clients get is not the "Push & Tell" treatment but the "Black Hole" treatment. Sometimes, the case is pushed, sometimes it isn't. Sometimes, whether the case is pushed or not, the "Tell" is missing. Being a client and not knowing where your case is up to is a horrible feeling.

Clients suffer because their file is sat on the desk of a very busy lawyer who can never get around to working on it. Or they suffer because they have no idea where their case is up to, even when they call their lawyer as they never get a call back.

If you have never been the client engaged in what is for you a hugely emotive and important case, you will have no idea what it is like waiting for a call, not getting a call, and then not getting your calls returned. It is truly sickening.

Consider a lawyer who works all night drafting complex documents for a corporate client and who emails hundreds of pages of re-drafts to the client at 5 am the following morning with an email saying, "Latest drafts attached – comments?"

To the lawyer, that will feel like amazing service – "I worked until 5 in the morning!"

To the client (who is, of course, still trying to run a business), that is a nightmare. I know – the client in question was me.

Or consider the Private Client lawyer who spends weeks (and lots of chargeable hours) crafting a thesis that analyses a complex family legal situation. It gets sent to a client weeks later and leaves the client staring at the long letter in one hand, wondering what it's about, and a big bill in the other hand, wondering what they've got for the money, and unsure as to what they do next.

As part of assessing whether a lawyer is delivering a great service and making the clients feel better rather than worse, I always apply what I call the "Mum and

Dad" test. My Mum and Dad are very bright and "savvy", but watching them as business owners try to understand letters they'd received from their *own* solicitors was painful.

Many a lawyer that I have worked with has had letters that I found on the printer thrust back at them with the comment, "My Mum and Dad wouldn't have a clue what that letter was saying".

Of course, you never see law firms saying, "Our service is dreadful". On the contrary, "Great Service" is a regular law firm boast. But I simply do not believe that firms can easily deliver on a promise of "we will *always* deliver a great service".

Across all my dealings with lawyers in my personal, family, wider family, and business lives, I've never come across a *firm* that gets over this high bar. Individual lawyers *sometimes* can, but never a whole firm.

It is usually an empty boast, but it is empty for understandable reasons. It may be that a client used Lawyer A in a firm, and the service on that occasion was great. That might lead the client to use Lawyer A again if the same expertise is needed later.

But Lawyer A might be busier by then. They might be ill. They might be on holiday. They might be tied up in a big case for weeks, unable to give real attention to anything else.

Unless *Lawyer A's team and the whole firm* has systems and monitoring and resources in place to make sure that the clients of Lawyer A will not be kept waiting or kept in the dark about their case (whatever is going on in the business or personal life of Lawyer A) then the firm simply cannot boast that they always provide a great service.

My point here is that, on their own, with the best will in the world, a lawyer simply *cannot* deliver on a promise that they will always deliver a great service. But it is not just *their* problem – it is the *team's* and, therefore, the *firm's* challenge. The firm cannot bark at lawyers and say, "You've always got to deliver a knockout service" – it's simply not possible. An all-team and all-firm commitment is what is needed.

This challenge becomes even clearer if the client is so impressed with Lawyer A (who is, say, dealing with Matter .001 for a new client) that the client approaches Lawyer A with a *different* type of case they need help with. As this new case is outside Lawyer A's expertise, Lawyer A would have to pass it to Lawyer B in another team, who opens up Matter .002 for that client.

But is Lawyer B overwhelmed, too? Is any culture, system, protocol, commitment, training, reward, team effort, monitoring, management, sense of pride, or accountability structure in place to ensure that the lawyers across *all the teams* deliver a great service, so that the client gets a great service there, too, and a great service is delivered by every lawyer, *every team*, every time?

It's only if *that* all exists that the client will keep coming back so that they clock up more and more matters with the firm, taking their Client Matter printout beyond .001 and .002, up to .003, .004, .005, .006, and .007.

In Business Development terms, getting to .007 is nirvana – it is a licence to bill.

Sadly, these things are not usually in place. Many of the boasts that are made by firms around "service" would not stand up to even the simplest form of scrutiny. Scrutiny such as, "Okay – you say your service levels are always excellent. Tell me how you ensure that lawyers in your Employment team, your Property team, and your Litigation team all deliver a great service, regardless of what cases or piles of files the lawyers have on their desks?" Not many law firms can give a compelling answer to this question.

This is a shame. Bad for clients and bad for business. History is littered with examples of one lawyer in one team impressing a client so that the client brought more work-types to the firm, only for lawyers in other teams to fail to ring the client back, or to bill the life out of the job, or to put the file into storage.

Law firms may say, "We check inactivity reports, so we know when a file has not been worked on". Maybe, but all that has to happen for a file not to appear on an inactivity report is a lawyer spending one unit on it. (The dreaded "one unit"!).

One unit doesn't always take a case forwards, so the client is sat waiting for progress at a time when all looks well from the firm's perspective.

(It's an incomplete solution, but at the very least, it might be better to tailor your inactivity reports so that they report on files that have not had at least one hour spent on them in the last month. A month is an incredibly long time in the life of a client with a matter that is of huge importance to them. As is a week.)

So, what can be done to build up a meaningful, high-quality, sustainable, service-based differentiator for a law firm?

1. A Service Pledge

The first thing that is needed by lawyers and law firms who are committed to moving towards "Perfect" status is the design of a Service Pledge that suits them, their resources, and their personality, and on which they are committed to delivering all of the time.

Sometimes, this begins with a short and simple set of promises, which can then be developed further over time.

The main thing is to arrive at a promise that the whole firm will absolutely keep all the time. Authenticity, not hot air, is the name of the game here.

We need the whole firm (for it is the whole firm, not just the lawyers, that delivers the service) to look at what makes good service and what makes bad service. And not from their perspective, but from a client's perspective.

I usually do this in law firms by giving groups (each made up of a mix of lawyers and Business Support staff) an imaginary scenario where I – as a client – am in an urgent, complex, difficult position. Just as our clients often are.

Dividing each group into two imaginary law firms, I ask one firm – Bad & Co – to plot what they will do to deliberately turn my already difficult position into an absolute catastrophe for me.

I ask the other "firm" – Good & Co – to describe how they will move heaven and earth to get me through my predicament and to a sound resolution.

Starting with Bad & Co, we record and map out what foul and evil works they come up with. It usually looks like this:

BAD & CO	GOOD & CO (Just insert the opposite!)
Take the case on, even though it's not something you've done much of	
Pass the file to a junior lawyer	
Don't communicate with the client	
Don't keep the client updated	
Don't acknowledge receipt of anything	
Don't return the client's calls	
Don't stick to deadlines	
Only work on this file when you have to	
Never really get into the detail	
Quote £5,000 and bill £10,000	

Pass the file between lawyers, all of whom bill "reading in" time	

The amazing and absolutely horrifying thing is that if you look at what the lawyers at Bad & Co usually come up with – when they have been asked to do their very worst for a client-in-need – they come up with the very things that clients actually complain of!

Many of them are things that I have personally experienced over the years, and that many people with whom I have talked have also experienced.

From this, you can see that it's not hard to arrive at a series of simple promises to clients about what you will do, and what you will not do, when you deal with any case for them in *any part* of your firm.

You can thus arrive at a firm-wide Service Pledge that your whole firm has designed and that all of your people believe in. Your Service Pledge is something that prospective clients will very much like the sound of, because they've often had bad experiences with lawyers in the past. It will mean that clients will choose you – and then stay with you and use you (and your colleagues) – for more and more legal work. Without looking at the price.

I still love (and am still very proud of) the story of the discerning, High Net Worth, CEO, and multiple business-owning client who asked me why he should use my firm for his wide-ranging legal needs.

I literally said only five words.

Try it. Good luck.

In response to my five words, he replied, "I'm all yours".

My five words were, "Have a look at that".

"That" was our list of differentiators, the first of which was our cross-firm commitment to giving "A great service – every lawyer, every time". Those were the very words we used – they were splashed around our office walls.

You can see how "service" as a differentiator is compelling. It gets potential clients (who usually dread the thought of using lawyers again) to become actual clients. At a higher price.

It goes much, much further than that, though. When it comes to Matter .001, all you are really getting is a first chance to impress the client. You then have to deliver on the "service" differentiator you boasted of, if you are to move over time towards .007.

I can demonstrate this with reference to the same discerning client mentioned just above, with his complex family and business lives and the recurring need he and they had for a broad range of legal services.

He grew from Matter .001 into a large personal, family, and corporate client that gave work to a good number of personal and business teams across my firm.

When I mentioned to him a year down the road that we'd won his work with just five words, his canny reply was that no, we hadn't. We'd won *the first case* with those five words, but all the other cases had been won because of *four* other words. Wow! This was an incredible discussion for me.

His four words? Verbatim? "You give a shit".

He explained that *every* lawyer that he ever dealt with at my firm delivered an exceptional service. He said there was a clear "way" that we *all* did things – whatever the lawyer's seniority.

He said that everyone he had ever dealt with at my firm delivered the same great service, and that during a lifetime of using lawyers around the world as part of his business, he had never seen anything like it. He could see that it was no accident.

He said that he was no longer bothered about the price. Significantly, he also mentioned that everyone he ever referred to us reported the same phenomena to him. He was in our Sales Team.

A Service Pledge can win you new clients who will pay you a high price. Delivering on it constantly will grow the value of those clients to your business. And it'll be a recruiting sergeant for your sales team.

2. Get those hands up!

The second thing that's needed to enable a firm to really deliver a great service – every lawyer, every time – though, is an ethos where everyone is empowered (indeed *proud*) to put their hands up whenever they feel they are *not* delivering on the firm's Service Pledge.

Failure needs to be built into the system, otherwise the system will fail. Here, identifying failure is a success.

A lawyer putting their hand up in this way to their line manager is to be celebrated – it shows the system is working. It is a "learning" moment. Lawyers might see it as a failure, but commerce and industry "out there" see such things as a success. We must, too.

The challenge is then passed up the line until a solution to the challenge is found. That solution often consists of reallocating work within a team or – if all "vessels" are full – recruiting more lawyers.

Where this opportunity to truly build a brand breaks down is when a lawyer cannot get around to working on all the files that they have, and either:

- they do not feel comfortable putting their hand up in this way (maybe because they fear that it will be seen as a sign of weakness), or

- they want to keep all their files on their own desk so they can hit their individual billing target, or

- they see the client as *their* client, or

- they don't trust their colleagues, or

- they do put their hands up, but nothing happens

3. Rewarding "service"

The third thing that is needed here is a commitment by Management that the firm's resources will be applied to encourage the entire firm to work to this Service Pledge.

Embracing and delivering on the Service Pledge should be key factors in the appraisal process, the promotion process, and – of course – the induction process. Anyone who helps the firm as a whole to deliver on the Pledge or to build an even stronger Pledge, ought to be seen as someone as valuable as a good biller. Good billers are often celebrated, with a blind eye being turned to other, destructive impacts.

Anyone (whoever they are, and however senior they are, and however much they bill) who does not buy into the Service Pledge and who continues to exhibit non-Pledge behaviours (which could be as simple as never returning calls) has to be seen as someone who is undermining your whole brand. That will cost you a fortune.

The Team Leaders and the Partners in the firm have to lead the way and lead by example. If they turn a blind eye, how can you expect people under them to work to build your brand and the value of your business?

4. Teamwork and Delegation

The fourth internal thing that is needed is teamwork and delegation. We could call it vessel-filling.

Good lawyers at good firms are *always* busy. They'll literally *never* have an empty desk, so they'll literally *never* be able to give a case their full time and attention without having to put another file to the back of the desk.

But there is a way to achieve consistent service excellence, and to deliver on your brand in a way that makes profit, however many new files come in.

Consider the position of senior Lawyer A in a firm who charges, say, £300 an hour and who works as an island with no support from any junior lawyers. Let's say that they usually record 5 chargeable hours a day (that's high!).

If a new file then comes to Lawyer A – perhaps as a result of the firm's marketing activity and spend, or as a result of Lawyer A's profile because they are "the best" – then unless Lawyer A starts doing 6 or 7 chargeable hours a day or working weekends, there's going to be absolutely no financial gain in the short or medium term to the firm as a result of that new case coming in. What was the point of getting it?

What will probably happen is that Lawyer A will push the current case they're working on to the back of the desk, and they'll start working instead on the new case.

They'll do the same number of chargeable hours a day.

And whereas, before, the firm was earning £300 an hour, it has got in a great new case, and it is now earning, well, £300 an hour still.

And one happy client (who may be the client of another team in the firm) is now shortly going to become an unhappy client – along with all the others that are already at the back of the desk.

As you can see, under this way of working, there is simply no way that Lawyer A can deliver on a Service Pledge to always "Push & Tell".

And the firm is losing out on money – lots of it.

Now, consider another way of doing things. Let's look at Lawyer B, who works at The Perfect Legal Business. At this firm, each senior lawyer has support from one or more junior lawyers. Crucially – they have support from junior lawyers that they *trust*.

Suitably trained in the art of delegation and charged with (and rewarded for) filling the vessels below (i.e., the desks of their junior lawyers), rather than just being charged with hitting a personal billing target, Lawyer B's focus can always be on getting a file into a position where a "lieutenant" lawyer can take it over, under their ongoing supervision.

Where this happens, Lawyer B charges £300 for their senior expertise on a file, then passes the file to the lieutenant lawyer, who subsequently charges £200 for their more junior input on that file, while Lawyer B gets on with senior work on *another* file. And maybe very junior work on the file is passed to a paralegal at £100 an hour. With all three tiers of lawyer working on different tasks, and with those files all getting lawyers' attention rather than being sat at the back of a desk, the firm can now be billing – across the various different cases – *£600* an hour. It was now well worth the firm getting a new case in.

And no one is happier than the client. The client is benefitting in not just one but two genuine and indisputably important ways:

- First, their case is being pushed, not stored
- Second, junior work is being done at junior rates

That brings both service excellence and value for money (as well as maximum short-term profit for the firm).

There is a huge gulf between the experience of the client using Lawyer A and that of the client using Lawyer B. And the latter's firm is making far more money.

There is something you can do, as well, which not only advertises the fact that there is something different about your firm and that the genuine difference is quality of service, but it also allows you to ensure that you are actually delivering on your promise/brand at all times. This is the gathering of *real-time* client feedback and responsive quality control.

Do you ask your clients for feedback on your service level? Some firms do. Often, it's a case of sometimes. Some lawyers, in some teams, in some firms, send a questionnaire out to some clients at the end of some cases, or the end of the year.

Other firms are more military and thorough about it, where *every* client gets a questionnaire at the end of every case, across the firm.

It's still all long after the horse (or, rather, the client) may have bolted.

Having committed ourselves to delivering "A great service – every lawyer, every time" at my firm, we wanted to go further than this. We wanted to know that we were actually delivering a great service – every lawyer, every time – *as each case progressed.*

It wasn't enough for us to find out at the end of a case that the client hadn't been happy. We wanted *real-time* quality control and brand measurement.

We had built failure into our system here, too, in that we felt sure we would sometimes fail, but if we caught failure quickly and before things deteriorated, we could get things back on track with a client.

At the time, no software existed (as it does now) that made this easy or indeed possible. Our superb IT team, however, came to the rescue in designing and building the "ABC Text" system that we launched.

Every time a file was opened for any client, we explained to them our commitment to delivering a great service – every lawyer, every time – and we asked them if they'd work with us to make sure we delivered on that promise. They were always very happy to.

At intervals that the client chose *during their case* (weekly, fortnightly, or monthly), our system automatically sent them a text simply asking if our service was A (Great) or B (Okay) or C (Poor). If anyone replied with a "C", I as Managing Partner, would ring them.

I rang a few such clients and the impact was always the same – sheer astonishment that anything at all came from their reply, let alone a call from the Managing Partner. Unhappy clients became not just happy clients, but amazed, loyal, evangelical clients.

No lawyers or teams could (or wanted to) opt out. The results were gathered centrally and shared internally. The results were also published on the homepage of our website. That's brave!

This system allowed us to constantly identify where we had turned into a storage business instead of a legal business – where we were failing to deliver on our pledge to clients. We could identify files that needed an hour, but were only getting a unit when something urgent happened instead.

The client and the business would benefit if all files that needed such time got it.

And while we're talking about "one unit", consider the impact of this system on a client's case and a client's bills when it is employed by an over-busy lawyer.

From a client's perspective, the whole "unit" system can work – unless lawyers are too busy. Then the "*unit*" system turns into the "*one unit*" system. It can then be devastating in ways that lawyers typically don't realise or care about.

One unit can be valuable – a key (short) letter, for example. Having been the client of many a law firm, though, I can tell you that "one unit" is often *not* very valuable – particularly when several people spend "one unit" discussing the file, and they all record the time. One unit is 6 minutes, but it's usually recorded because someone – or several people – has spent one minute (or less) on a file.

As a client, when you ask for a time printout and you see that high cost levels have been run up, it is often a build-up not of units but of "*one units*" by one or more people. There is often ample justification for a client to question the value for money they have received in such cases. The costs shoot up while the file goes nowhere because one or more lawyers have often been snatching "one unit" to put out a fire.

(Did I mention the one and only firm I've worked with that charged *by the minute*? Now that's a differentiator.)

Another benefit, therefore, of lawyers being able to work on files when they need good time investing in them is that whilst the bills may be no lower – and may indeed be higher – there is material progress on the file and the client, therefore, sees and feels value for money.

You get a lot more progress on a file if a lawyer spends ten units on it as opposed to ten "one units".

In short, having been on the thick end of poor service from law firms, it seems to me that "Management" is often happy to boast about "excellent service" but hasn't really thought about what is needed to make sure that their lawyers can actually deliver on that promise.

A lawyer cannot make the boast that The Perfect Lawyer would aspire to – that they will always deliver a great service – without their team and their firm building the apparatus around them that enables this.

To jump out of the legal sector to reinforce my point, it's like a restaurant owner who spends a fortune designing and building an eye-catching venue, hiring a Michelin chef, designing a stunning menu, winning awards, and making a lot of noise on social media – but who doesn't have enough serving staff on the floor at all, let alone serving staff who have the right "customer experience" training.

What happens? There is no warm welcome for customers, they get ignored when they walk in for their special and expensive night out, they wait ages to even get a drink, they start feeling tense and bad about the night instead of good, the food is cold, and they generally have no one looking after them. They might even have trouble paying at the end of the night.

On paper, the food might be amazing, and the whole restaurant venue, too, but the overall *experience* is poor because the staff have got too many tables to look after and the whole customer experience thing was never properly walked through.

I've been to restaurants like this. I've seen all those things. I know how I talk about them after the event – I certainly don't join what should be their ever-growing salesforce. I've had the same experience with law firms.

Most adults have used a lawyer, but not many have *got* a lawyer. This is why. The technical law is rarely lacking, but the "client experience" often is.

I believe that this whole question of "service" is critical to The Perfect Legal Business and to clients having The Perfect Lawyer, as this is the key to building a true legal *brand*, to creating a real differentiator, to developing clients, and to earning a lifetime's value out of them (and their families and their friends).

It is the difference between a law firm that changes lives and one that sells t-shirts.

And, being blunt, it is also the key to getting clients to take their eye off the "price" ball.

And to getting your clients to do your marketing for you, to boosting the effectiveness of your own marketing, to growing your profitability and your cash reserves, and to being a legal business that you and your people can be absolutely proud of.

All too often, I have spoken with lawyers who are not proud of what they themselves do – their heart is in the right place but they're simply too busy to give clients a good, proactive service.

Nor are they always proud of what their colleagues do – some lawyers would still rather send a client to another firm than to their colleague down the corridor whose service level they simply don't trust.

The way out of this may surprise you. I have seen it so many times. Client satisfaction and client loyalty, and the right kind of financial growth, comes where caseloads go down and where a firm gets more lawyers in, not more cases. More "marketing" is not the way to secure growth.

I have seen teams in my firm, and teams that I have worked with at other firms, grow profitably without a single extra case coming in, where more lawyers are recruited, cases are distributed, and individual caseloads go down.

This action and courage on the part of a law firm allows Perfect Lawyers to emerge and to thrive, and – in turn – to make the law firm a Perfect Legal Business. It is an investment with a very healthy return.

Spending more time on fewer cases, where lawyers can all deliver on a firm's Service Pledge, where more time is spent on each file, more time is captured, and less time is lost by lawyers dashing from file to file to file, is good for everyone – in the short term and the long term.

In The Perfect Legal Business, service, client satisfaction, profit, cash, and growth are close bed-fellows.

CHAPTER 2

GETTING ALL THE WORK
A CLIENT HAS

Not only is a Service Pledge a differentiator that a law firm can wield "out there" to help it attract and convert more new clients and at a higher price, it is also the basis of the next thing that The Perfect Legal Business, and its Perfect Lawyers, strive to achieve.

Every client will have a need for additional and different legal services at some time or other. They are a client, not a case.

Getting all of that work, and extending maximum care, is the next dimension of The Perfect Legal Business and of The Perfect Lawyers within it.

Imagine a healthy tree – a trunk with various branches coming off it. That represents your typical client. Each branch is an area of law in which a law firm might be able to extend care to a personal or business client over the years. Now, let's imagine that this tree telephones a law firm with, say, an Employment issue.

It is irrelevant here whether the client is a personal client or a corporate client – the client is inevitably going to need a range of legal expertise over the coming years. And both types are clients are where a law firm can be proactive in extending care to them as well as being there reactively for them when anything "legal" arises.

During that first call to a law firm, that tree/client will utter a single word that will have a huge impact. They will mention "Employment".

Immediately, it will be as if the tree has been put into one of those de-branching machines so that all that is left is one branch. That branch will be sent through to the Employment team, where it will land on the desk of an Employment lawyer. The rest of the branches are sawdust.

The client is immediately "owned" by the lawyer on whose desk the case lands. No one else in the firm will ever come to know about them.

If that lawyer moves other files to the back of the desk so they can deal with the new file, and/or if they have no "Pride in Pricing" and/or no "Cash Commitment" – see Part 2 of this book – then it does not follow that this client is even going to help the firm grow its profit and cash reserves as it needs to.

If that lawyer already has a heavy caseload, and they are already struggling to deal with all the files they have on their desk, they are going to be unable to even do the work, let alone deliver the kind of service that will keep this new client happy. Their service to other clients will also deteriorate.

The outcome might very well be that even if the lawyer can keep the case and get to the end of it, the firm won't bill enough, won't get paid quickly enough, won't earn any additional profit, and the client won't be back for more if any other legal need crops up.

This happens thousands of times, and this is why – in my view – every adult and every business has *used* a lawyer, but many do not *have* a lawyer.

And all the while, the firm's Private Client Team, Property Team, Dispute Resolution Team, etc., are having meetings to discuss how they can get new clients. All the clients they need are already in the house!

The Perfect Legal Business and its Perfect Lawyers recognise the opportunity that the tree discussed above offers to the business. They don't see the tree as just the one branch – rather, they see the tree as a tree, with many branches, which are all opportunities to extend care to a client, for good fees, over time.

They see a new client's Matter .001 not as a short-term billing opportunity for one lawyer in one team, but as the first step in a long journey towards Matter .007 and beyond, for that client.

That journey leads to comfort and protection for the client, and it leads to sustained and easy profit, cash, and pride for the law firm. It also brings the client into your sales team.

What does The Perfect Legal Business and its lawyers do when it comes to engaging with a client? How does it move away from the department-based method of client engagement described above? What could it do that gets it off on an altogether different footing with every client?

Although (as will be clear from this book) my previous firm was far from being The Perfect Legal Business, as with the whole service ethos, differentiators, and brand-building, this was another area where we showed courage and imagination, and where we saw real impact and success.

In my firm, clients didn't just come onto one lawyer's desk or into one team – they came into the centre. Into one of two schemes, or "client clubs".

If they were individuals or families, they came into the central scheme or club that we set up for them. If they were a business client, they came into the business scheme or business club.

We also, of course, tried to get the *owners* of business clients to join the personal scheme – they're people after all, with quite complex personal legal needs. There was always a great opportunity to extend care to them – including proactively – to help them avoid issues later.

The engagement with clients was central. No individual or team owned the client – the commonwealth did. We all did. At one stage, I recall we had some 20,000 people in the personal scheme and about 1,000 businesses in the corporate scheme. The whole messaging and engagement here was deeper than just being about the case that the client brought to us.

A small but meaningful difference can be seen in the first letters that we sent out to new clients:

- Most firms write to their client saying "Dear X, re your Employment case" or "Dear Y, re Purchase of 23 Laburnam Lane".

- Our letters began, "Dear X, Welcome to the world of care that we offer to you, your family, and your business – now and in the future".

The clients of The Perfect Legal Business have to be owned by everyone. The Perfect Lawyer recognises that to truly care for a client, they cannot solely own that client.

A lawyer shielding a client from other colleagues and teams may preserve that lawyer's billings – and keep the client safe for when the lawyer starts going for interviews at other firms. But it is a very one-dimensional way of looking after a client. It is not, in fact, looking after a client at all.

There is a central engagement and a universal commitment to looking after all clients in "the PLB Way" that will benefit clients and all colleagues, not just a particular lawyer's own billing target. It's not about billing, and it's not about selling. It's about caring and it's about pride. Dual pride. The money will follow.

Our schemes and clubs came with a range of benefits for the clients. Not least, once you were a client of ours, we were all part of "being there" for all the firm's clients, so they could speak to any of our lawyers if any new legal matter arose in their personal or business life.

We used these schemes or "clubs" as a springboard to client nurturing and development – building on the "you are centrally owned and cared for" message that we'd sent out to clients from the outset.

For example, where a client business was of sufficient size, one of our "ambassadors" would visit them to get to know them in a non-sales way, and to explore opportunities for us to extend proactive care to them. The message to the clients was strong and long-lasting, and the ambassadors frequently came back with more opportunities for us to extend care (including proactively) to clients. This was our (very effective) form of Key Account Management.

I now work with law firms to set up these schemes or clubs, along with building the "service" differentiator, as part of a wider programme to move them towards being The Perfect Legal Business. Change, and at a pace, really is possible, if you can get over the obstacles…

Going back to the case of the tree, above, in The Perfect Legal Business, neither the Employment lawyer nor the Employment Team own the client. Rather, they are just carrying the baton for the time being.

While the Employment Team carries the baton on that client's Matter .001, the Employment Team's job – and in particular the Employment Team Leader's job – is to make sure the Employment lawyer who is dealing with the case delivers a great service in accordance with the firm's Service Pledge. That's how they do their bit for the whole firm. And everyone in all the other teams is doing the same thing for every client they are dealing with. It's one big team effort. Thus, they're all selling each other to all clients.

The individual Employment lawyer's job here is either to do a great job – to "Push and Tell" – or to put their hand up within their team and to their Team Leader if they are ever unable to push or tell. That will ensure that the Employment Team will deliver on the promise and keep Matter .001, and it will make sure the client considers the firm to be their lawyers should they need anything else.

It will also make them amenable to exploring the proactive care that The Perfect Legal Business extends to all of its clients, which I call "the platforms".

You can hopefully see a list of differentiators building up here that can set a law firm apart from the herd. We actually did all of this, and it worked.

First, we offered "a great service – every lawyer, every time". We all gave a shit.

Second, we offered the central engagement and the "client clubs" or schemes, which came with a range of benefits for personal or business clients. Already, that list is better than "We are award-winning" and "We are a Top 100 firm".

But there's more, because thirdly, we offered *proactive* care, rather than just waiting for the phone to ring.

While any team is carrying the baton for a client of the firm, and while the firm is therefore delivering an amazing service, so far that's a reactive service – responding to a call made by the client.

In a law firm, depending on the expertise you have under your roof and depending on relationships you have with other trusted law firms, there may be an opportunity to extend *proactive* care to personal and/or corporate clients.

CHAPTER 3

PROACTIVE CARE

The Perfect Lawyer is keen to make sure that clients of the firm (note that I didn't say *"their* clients") have all the protection that they and their colleagues might be able to put in place, as opposed to them solely owning a client and not letting other lawyers near them.

Keeping a client to yourself, waiting for them to ring you to use your narrow expertise again, and not letting your colleagues add value to them, could be putting your clients at risk.

A further thing The Perfect Legal Business and its team do, having engaged with a client in a central way, is *not* wait for the phone to ring.

We could doom this part of the project to failure by calling it "cross-selling". It's not selling – it's cross-*caring*.

At law firms I work with, I often ask the Matrimonial or Corporate or Conveyancing or Real Estate etc., lawyers in the room whether they care for their clients. They usually reply emphatically that they do.

I then ask them whether they have ever discussed with their business clients, for example, what would happen if a director or the CEO died, or more likely these days, they had a heart attack so that they were alive but without the legal capacity to run their personal or business affairs. What would happen to their business, its employees, the director's family, and so on?

In England (and many other countries have similar arrangements), if there is no Lasting Power of Attorney in place, the only thing the family can do is apply to the Court of Protection for someone to be appointed as what is called a "Deputy", so that the Deputy can then run the affairs of the affected person. That will cost many times what an LPA would have cost, and it can take a year to be processed. And there are ongoing costs and delays when you are dealing with the Court of Protection.

All the while, the family and the business are in limbo. This is trauma heaped on trauma. This could all be so easily avoided, and it is within the power of a lawyer to truly help clients here – to literally change their family and business lives. This could be done by harnessing the expertise of a firm's in-house Private Client team, or by working with trusted, external Private Client lawyers.

Many corporate and commercial lawyers have admitted to me that they have literally *never, ever* asked any of the hundreds of directors they have worked with whether they have all of the available and necessary protections in place. It had never occurred to them to do so. Or they didn't want to be seen to be *selling* to their clients.

Whilst many firms can point to a paragraph in the letter they send to Conveyancing clients, which says, "You need a Will", that's about as far as it goes – there is no centralised and cross-firm passion for actually *caring* for clients' wider well-being.

That's not "caring for clients". That's "making a buck". It's shallow. It's leaving clients exposed to monumental risks.

I think there is a real need and an opportunity here, in relation to personal clients and business owners, all of whom face the possibility of death with intestacy and/or loss of mental capacity.

- I have never once had a commercial lawyer say to me, "Yup – I do that as a matter of course".

- I have never yet seen a law firm that could say, "Yes – we do that with all of our clients, whichever team happens to be looking after them".

All individuals, adults, and families can be raised onto a platform where the risks they might otherwise face, or the impact of those risks, are reduced. All businesses and their owners can similarly be put on a platform where the risks they face, or the impact of those risks, are reduced. I believe there is a great opportunity for law firms to do something life-changing for clients – not by selling to them, but rather by proactively caring for them.

What is the alternative for clients? What do lawyers who do not care for their clients proactively, like this, leave their clients facing?

It could be that their wishes simply do not get put into effect if they die. The public takes all sorts of things for granted and lawyers can help them (proactively) to see if what they believe is actually accurate.

For example, in England, many a person has tried to leave a house to someone in a Will (e.g., to their new partner), only for it to transpire later that the property was still jointly owned with a third party (the former partner) so that on death (in this example) the former partner gets the whole property *regardless* of what the Will says. An exploration of the client's wishes and circumstances here would have shown that the Joint Tenancy in relation to that house had not been severed but needed to be. This is good fee-paying work that can quite literally change clients' lives!

That's if the person dies. It can be a whole lot worse if – as happens more and more – a person survives a catastrophic event but no longer has the mental capacity to look after their affairs. In such cases, in England, it's awful – years of dealing with the Court of Protection, waiting literally months for a reply, increased costs, and ongoing trauma whilst the family is all at sea, perhaps paralysed by an inability to access funds or to deal with property, care home fees, or business-related matters.

As I say above, I have seen how many firms write to conveyancing clients and to Matrimonial clients telling them that they should have a Will in place. And I have heard many firms talk about offering "free health checks" to businesses.

In spirit, these are both excellent initiatives and embody the approach of The Perfect Legal Business. Most of the time, though, I fear they can come across as less important and valuable to the client than they really could be. They are peripheral to the work being done for a client, not central to it, and their mention is fleeting.

Law firms are sat on life-changing and business-changing awareness, knowledge, and experience. The vast majority of that is only put at the disposal of clients when something hits the fan. That is a real shame and a missed opportunity.

We wanted to do something about it when I was Managing Partner. For personal clients, we developed something that we called The Portfolio. The Portfolio was a nice, branded box-file that was given to as many clients as possible. In it was a guide to the clear advantages for them of getting three vital pieces of paper in place:

- a Will

- a "Property & Financial" Lasting Power of Attorney

- a "Health" Lasting Power of Attorney.

We didn't *sell* these things. Instead, we educated clients about their value, and implored clients to get them in place, whether it was through our offices or those of another law firm. It was part of a joined-up, consistent message that we were on the same side as the client. Although there were pricing advantages for a client if they procured two or more of these documents, they weren't priced low. Our aim was to have clients get their Portfolios in place and all their affairs in order.

I recall one occasion when I was working with a law firm to build up a head of steam on this "proactive care" initiative. A lady in the group became very upset because – at that very time – her family was wrestling with all the ramifications of someone in her family having lost capacity without there being a Lasting Power of Attorney in place. Everything had to be done via the Court of Protection, where response times are measured in months, not hours or days. It reinforced my belief in all that I was doing.

Of course, going the extra mile by getting all your "people" clients to get their affairs in order is easy if you have a lawyer or lawyers under your roof who do that area of work. But what if you don't have a Private Client team? You have a choice, I believe:

- Ignore the whole opportunity to care and the whole opportunity to show your clients that you care

- Show them that you do care, by educating them about the risks they run and urging them to go to another law firm to get their affairs all sorted out

- Show them that you do care, but by working in collaboration with a trusted and non-competing law firm that *can* deliver these services. The clients are still educated on the risks they are running, and they will see that you care for them selflessly.

We did have a Private Client team at my firm so we were able to extend this care and expertise ourselves. We could thus add this proactive care to our list of differentiators, and I now help law firms to design and launch all of these differentiators, including what I have come to call these client "platforms". These are tailored to each firm and their expertise, their resources, and – of course – their clients.

Getting clients to "Portfolio" state is truly life-changing for them. My wife and I both still have our Portfolios on our shelf at home – everything is in order lest the worst happens. It'll save our kids and wider family a fortune in trauma, delay, and expense. It also allowed us to make some decisions that we wouldn't want any of our family to have to make.

For business clients, the opportunities to help your clients climb onto a platform where they are safer are all the greater. It takes the "free health check" idea and makes it actually happen, but as part of a constant and wider "care" message.

"Let us work with you to get you onto a platform where you'll pay lawyers a lot less and where your Management time can be spent on positive rather than negative things". Business clients will thank you for helping them get their account-opening procedures, terms and conditions, credit control system, shareholders agreement, and employment contracts, etc., all dove-tailed and up-to-date. At a price, of course.

These "platforms" are so many things at the same time – things to be proud of, things that can change clients' lives, differentiators in your marketplace, and generators of good fees. They are also "cement" between you and your clients.

Where these opportunities to care for clients and to bill for the benefit of the legal business can be extinguished is where lawyers take the view (and are allowed to take the view) that "My clients are my clients, and no one is *selling* anything to them". Individual fee targets and individual billing bonuses can reinforce this, as can a fear that the service levels of some teams are not up to scratch.

These views and these things have no place in The Perfect Legal Business and are not traits of The Perfect Lawyer. How can a lifetime's care, in the broadest sense, be offered and extended to a client who has very limited engagement with a firm?

Summary of Part 1

It is possible to provide a perfect legal service to clients all the time, but not even Perfect Lawyers can do it on their own.

A team of them can, in a framework, though, where the firm incentivises team behaviours and where failure is built into the system. And there needs to be a long-term commitment to all of this. "Flash in the pan" doesn't work and is a missed opportunity. Brands stick around. Or they're not brands.

I hope I have shown in Part 1 that not only do perfect law firms deliver a perfect service to clients – they go much further than that and help clients to get ahead of the curve and keep their trauma, anguish, and legal spend down.

If only that was all there was to being a Perfect Lawyer...

PART 2

FROM THE INTERNAL PERSPECTIVE – THAT OF THE LAW FIRM

CHAPTER 4

WHAT THE PERFECT LEGAL BUSINESS NEEDS FROM ITS LAWYERS

There's a lot more to the question of what makes up The Perfect Lawyer than just what clients think.

Lawyers do not exist in a vacuum. They are part of a firm.

A firm may have disciplines around, or requirements of, its lawyers. For example, it may be that the perfect lawyer in that firm goes into their real or home-based office every day and does nothing but records time and bills a fortune and who doesn't let anybody else in the firm talk to "my clients".

But in this book, we are not talking about what makes the perfect lawyer in any real-life firm. Instead, we are exploring what makes The Perfect Lawyer in The Perfect Legal Business.

The Perfect Legal Business is very often different to real-life law firms, many of which are missing huge opportunities to change clients' lives, to change the lives of their people, and to make maximum profits and cash. My first book, "The Perfect Legal Business" was all about what such a firm would look like.

What I describe here, in The Perfect Lawyer, cannot therefore be created in every law firm, as those firms stand. For The Perfect Lawyer to be at all possible, they need to be breathing in the air of a Perfect Legal Business.

Actually, it's a "chicken and egg" situation. If the lawyers behave in the ways that I describe here, the result will be that their firm will become a Perfect Legal Business. If a law firm is a Perfect Legal Business, its lawyers will be required to behave in the ways that I describe here.

Therefore, there is work to be done on the part of both the lawyer and the firm if we are to create the lawyer described in this book. A law firm cannot simply demand or expect that its lawyers become "perfect" as defined here – it has a part to play, too.

As such, this book is not a guide on how you get on (in career terms) in your law firm (though I bet some of the disciplines and behaviours we talk about here will help you to do just that). Rather, it is a guide as to how a law firm and its Management, on the one hand, and the lawyers who work in the firm on the other, can adopt certain priorities and behaviours, and can combine, where the outcome will be Perfect Lawyers in a Perfect Legal Business. You can't have the latter without the former. And the latter will constantly create more of the former. It is a sustainable spiral – upwards – and it is a great place to be.

So now, in Part 2 of this book, I look at what a law firm needs to do itself, and at what it needs from its lawyers, in order to achieve this happy state.

Whilst a lawyer might be very popular with clients, the needs of the law firm (and, more importantly, of the legal *business*) go much further than those of the clients – and may even conflict with them.

You can be everything *a client* has dreamt of in terms of a lawyer, but you are not an island. You are part of a legal business – a business that is under constant pressure to grow.

I look at all of this here, and I also look at what firms can do to bring out the best in their people and at how they might currently be bringing out the worst.

The only place where The Perfect Lawyer can exist is in a crucible where the right energy and commitment and attitude on an individual lawyer level is mixed with the right attitude and commitment on the part of Management. What we need here is a partnership where there is trust and pride and passion on both sides.

The lawyers in the firm cannot just plough their own furrow and do things their way. The firm needs them to get on board and exhibit team-like, selfless behaviours, and to strive for longer-term outcomes. The firm needs to identify, incentivise, and reward these behaviours rather than allowing and maybe even driving contrary ones.

Let's get started!

CHAPTER 5

WHAT THE PERFECT LEGAL BUSINESS NEEDS FROM ITS LAWYERS II

In looking at what The Perfect Lawyer is *to a law firm*, we need to first go back and look at the whole "clients" question further.

In Part 1 of this book, we focused on delivering to clients all that *they* wanted.

The first thing that a senior lawyer will tell a junior lawyer is that you need to be wary of the very people we have just spent so long talking about – clients.

Clients can be a mixed bag. They are an asset that can turn into a nightmare. Senior lawyers never forget that. We need to keep clients at a professional and healthy distance. Never let your guard down.

To recap on what clients want of their lawyers, the list generally includes the following positive attributes:

- My lawyer really knows their stuff

- They always take my call

- They've been around the block, and they've seen it all

- They are real fighters

- You'd rather have them on your side than against you

- They talk in plain English

- You never have to ring them – they always ring you

Not all clients are as straight or as scrupulous as you might like them to be. Some of the things such clients might like to see in their lawyer are not good:

- My lawyer does as I ask

- They bend the rules for me

- They're junior, so they don't stand up to me

- They're friendly – great fun on a night out after a few beers

- They're a pushover

- They're cheap

- They don't put a lot of the stuff they do "on the clock"

- You can ask them about other legal matters – they always help

- You can pay "on the drip"

What is perfect for a client is not always perfect for a lawyer or a law firm. It is a naïve and dangerous lawyer – a downright liability – who ticks all of the above boxes.

Having looked in Part 1 at what clients want from their lawyers, we need to be circumspect. Let's consider the approach that I believe a lawyer and a law firm should take in relation to clients.

This approach should apply to *all lawyers* in the firm regardless of who they are. No "big hitters" should be above or outside these rules. It would be insanity if lawyers across a law firm could take on whichever clients they want.

The damage a client can cause to a law firm is not always localised to the lawyer or the team that took them on, so no lawyer or team should be free to act as an island on this front. One lawyer in one team taking on a rogue client can lead to everyone's lights being switched off.

A lawyer in your firm who takes on any and every client without being fussy is anything but a success and an asset. Do not see them as one of those hallowed "rain-makers". Rain? They could well be brewing up a storm for the firm. I have seen this and learned this lesson to my great cost.

Let's look at what the business needs from its lawyers when it comes to who the firm's clients are.

Client selection and engagement

The Perfect Legal Business (and, therefore, The Perfect Lawyer) is fussy about who gets taken on as a client.

The Perfect Lawyer should be the guardian at the gate – not someone stood at the gate with open arms, welcoming everyone in. Clients bathe in the reflected glory of having your personal name and your firm's name behind them. You bring credibility to them. Don't let anyone have that advantage without you pausing and examining them and laying down some rules. A law firm – and a lawyer – should be very slow to take on any new client for two main reasons.

First, with clients come risks – reputational risks, risks of losing money on the case, risks of complaints, risks of adverse reviews on the internet, risks to your well-being, and risks of claims against your Professional Indemnity Insurance policy.

Of course, as with the start of any relationship, whilst clients love you at the outset, that doesn't always last. Wait until something costs them money. If you haven't yet had a client turn against you, it's only a matter of time! Weigh them up, don't go out and get drunk with them, never tell them anything about your personal life, and absolutely make a note of every bit of advice you ever give them.

I recall well the client I had when I was a young lawyer, who thought I was the best thing since sliced bread – until something went wrong in his case. Then he wrote directly to my Head of Department to say that I'd previously accepted a gift from him. Little did he know that at the time he gave me the gift, I'd immediately taken it to the Head of Department he was now writing to. Avoid such traps. Keep your distance – and keep your radar fully on.

Second, there is the risk that in adding them to an already great number of clients and files, you won't be looking after any of your clients in a way that would make your service level the powerful differentiator we looked at in Part 1 of this book, or in a way that will avoid complaints, or in a way that will help you and your colleagues to extend a lifetime's care to them.

Not only does The Perfect Legal Business know that the more clients you have, the less you can impress them with your service level and the more client issues you'll get (many of which will take considerable Management time to put to bed). It also knows that more and more clients and more and more files (to which more and more compliance demands get attached) will need more and more desks and IT equipment and a growing Business Support team.

It also knows that having an overwhelming number of files doesn't enhance a business; it can hinder it in direct financial terms as well as in staff well-being and wider "brand" terms. Having lots of files makes you very busy and on paper, therefore, more files should mean more profit, which would justify the increased spending on overheads across the firm.

Often, though, lawyers and firms are simply too busy to make as much money as they should. I see this in every firm I work with. Why do busy lawyers typically only record 3-4 chargeable hours a day, even though they're working far more hours than that, and even though the "unit" system of time recording means more time can literally be recorded than is actually spent?

Looking at time recording data, very many lawyers are being paid to do a full-time job, but you'd think that they are going home at lunchtime. They're obviously not, but one reason it looks like that is because they are running from pillar to post on their huge caseloads, unable to catch all the time they spend on files.

Frantic activity but poor time recording diminishes billing. So, individually and collectively, hard-working lawyers often do not get just financial desserts for their efforts and commitment.

As surprising as it may sound, "lots of files" increases overheads and can actually erode profit rather than increase it.

And what kind of service are lawyers providing as they run from pillar to post, as other files sit on the desk with even the most committed lawyers unable to get around to dealing with them at all (let alone dealing with them fully and properly)?

When I was a fee-earner, I had personal experience of passing a high number of my files to other lawyers in my team. I had put my hand up because I had far too many files and was sinking – and I was no less busy as a result of passing files around my colleagues. The files and clients I retained started getting a much better service. Those files that I distributed fared equally well. And the firm started making far more money out of what had been a caseload largely in storage.

I have lost count of the number of times when I have seen a new lawyer come into a team and be given cases that the existing lawyers effectively had in storage, where the outcomes were that every lawyer (new and old) remained busy throughout, *and billing and client satisfaction went up* – with no new cases coming in.

Firms ask me to help them to grow. But we rarely embark in the direction that they expect to start with. The first priority must always be to look at the files that are already open. If the lawyers have files that aren't being worked on properly, where time is being snatched when a client rings or a time limit approaches, why add more files to that pile?

There is plenty of money waiting to be made on the files that the firm already has. Let's get the existing files worked on properly. That usually means that a first step towards growth is to get more lawyers, not more files.

Another way of looking at this is to set a loose budget *for a file*. An experienced Team Leader will know, for example, that a divorce case of a particular size and nature should produce fees of, say, £10,000. If you give lawyers too heavy a caseload, they simply cannot give a file all the time it needs. The case will still progress, but the lawyer will be snatching time rather than working on the file thoroughly and proactively. The firm might get only £5,000 from the case and, of course, in terms of the work done, who knows what a snatched job will have missed compared to a thorough one.

It's a bizarre way of looking at it, I know, but often clients' biggest complaints are that their bills aren't big enough. I have felt this myself when I was a client, as discussed when I looked at the "one unit" issue in Chapter 1.

To make sure the clients get the service they want, and to make sure the firm generates maximum profit and cash, the key is not, therefore, to take on any and every new client or to have "hundreds of files" and massive lawyer caseloads.

Instead, there are three other keys:

- Ensure that individual lawyers don't have more cases than they can deal with properly and fully and in a thorough (rather than an urgent) fashion. This can be achieved by having more lawyers and spreading the cases around.

- Have a model where senior lawyers have good and trusted junior lawyer support, and the senior lawyers are charged with "filling the vessels" of their supporting lawyers and supervising their work on an ongoing basis. (Of course, individual billing targets – as opposed to team targets – will scupper the chances of this happening).

- Ensure that the firm simply does not take on all the cases that come knocking on its door. Only good cases for good clients that together offer good profit, and soon, with quick payment, should be taken on. This is achieved by the lawyers all setting a number of rules, or bars, that every client and case has to get over.

In short, I am an advocate of filtering out clients so that a lawyer can *do less, better.*

Here are my suggested rules that a lawyer should apply whenever they are looking at a new client, to raise the bar.

Rule 1 – Is this case in an area of law where I have real expertise?

Many a Professional Negligence claim against a law firm has arisen as a result of a lawyer or law firm "dabbling".

If you are not steeped in a particular work-type and you come up against a lawyer who is, you (and your client) are at real risk.

When I was a specialist Commercial Litigation solicitor, I saw on many occasions how a detailed knowledge of the rules gave me and my client a distinct advantage over general practitioners who didn't have the luxury of spending all their time with their heads in specialist litigation books. It was like taking candy off a baby sometimes. That was before the advent of the legion of online resources that are now available, so it can only have got much worse since I was a lad.

Be brave and say no – and I don't mean even when there's a big case and a big fee up for grabs. I mean *particularly* when there's a big case and a big fee up for grabs. Just say no.

There can be other benefits of taking such an approach. I recall an AIM-listed corporate client for whom I was the Client Partner and with whom there was a great relationship. Over time, we got all their work except their "Listed" work, as they used a City firm for that. One day, they asked me if we could act for them in a large corporate acquisition. In conjunction with our Corporate team (who strongly believed that we did not have the resources of a City firm, so we should not take the case on), we told the client that they would be better served by using their current lawyers on that job. The clients were bowled over by our honest, selfless response – and it took the relationship to an even higher plain.

Further in this vein, I once spent some quality time with an inspiring lawyer who could teach us all a good lesson. He had long been the typical busy High Street lawyer taking on anything that came through his door. He was being run off his feet, was not able to deliver a service he was at all proud of, wasn't a real expert in all of the areas he was dealing with (so he did a lot of "dabbling"), and he wasn't making anything like the money his high activity and stress levels warranted.

He decided to focus on one area, and to turn away every other work-type that he was constantly trying to get to grips with. He explained to me that all he did now was Residential Conveyancing, and he sent all Matrimonial, Motoring, Private Client, etc., cases to a firm down the road.

Not only did he reduce risk in this way. He now did Conveyancing *at a high hourly rate* – no fixed-fee quotes from him.

We compared my (expensive) city centre firm's scale fees against some "actuals" that he had recently charged. His fees were literally over double ours. And he was busy. Very. And clients referred clients to him. If they wanted a fixed-price quote, he just told people he didn't do them. Sounds amazing, doesn't it? But then he asked me this question:

Him: "How long have you been here this morning?"

Me: "About 40 minutes."

Him: "Have you heard the phone ring?"

Me: "No."

Him: "It rarely does – because I ring everyone. All the time. Every day. No one ever has to ring me. I push everyone and I get conveyances completed quicker than clients have ever seen before. I stick to what I'm good at, my service is phenomenal, and I charge properly for it".

He had not only stopped "dabbling", he was happier, more proud, making more money, and delivering a better service than ever before. This is a great example of a lawyer *doing less, better, for more.*

Rule 2 - Don't compete on price

The second rule I advocate is that lawyers should have "Pride in Pricing". Say it loud – "We are dear!" But on its own, that's not enough. If you can't justify *why* you are dear and perhaps dearer than your competitors, why would someone pay more to use you?

Lots of law firms talk on their website about being "competitively priced". Why? Is your service and expertise no better than anyone else's?

The Perfect Legal Business and its lawyers are able to say, "We're dear *because we have real differentiators, but they come at a price*".

In the story about the conveyancer above, what he was actually saying was, "I'm different. I charge double what my competitors charge, but cast your mind back to the last house move you were involved in. Remember when no one called you back? Recall not knowing whether or when you were going to be moving, and not knowing whether or when you should arrange the removal company for? Remember not having a clue where anything was up to, or not understanding what any blockage was, or how any blockage would be resolved? Remember pulling your hair out? You avoid all of that with me, but you've got to pay for it".

If a firm can truly embrace the service ethos in a concrete way (and create a working environment where its lawyers can truly deliver on it rather than being crushed with huge caseloads), there is a real business dividend available. "We're dearer because you will benefit from our Service Pledge. It's on our website – have a look. We all work to it. It essentially means we *always* push your case and we *always* tell you where your case is up to". Clients will pay good money for that.

If the whole firm is delivering a great service, changing clients' lives for the better, every time, that is something that everyone in the firm can really be proud of – for it is an achievement indeed.

Hand in hand with that pride, though, must go what I call "Pride in Pricing". If you are doing something amazing, don't give it away. Don't charge Volkswagen prices for a Bentley-level service. We need parallel pride – pride in what you are doing for the clients, and pride in what you are doing for *the business*.

A Real Estate Partner at a firm I was working with said he was facing a "new client" issue at that very moment. A property developer had asked him how much he'd charge for (I think) a lease renewal. The Partner told him, "£1,650 plus VAT". The client replied that if the lawyer would do it for £850, the lawyer could have all his lease work. I asked the lawyer what his reply would have been if we hadn't been looking at the whole service level and "Pride in Pricing" topic. He said he'd have done it cheap and celebrated winning all the client's work.

And now? The Partner went back to the developer and explained that he and this firm did things a certain way, delivering an excellent service, and that the firm didn't want *any* of his work, let alone all of it, if the price was just £850.

They won that job at £1,650, and then the rest of the client's work, too, on the strength of the Partner's initial self-worth and the high-quality service he then delivered.

Rule 3 – Define what you are doing (and what you are not doing) for the client

In short, define your retainer very carefully in the client care letter at the outset. There are two reasons for this.

First, the Professional Indemnity Insurance reason. Many a PII insurer has paid out where a client suffered a loss and blamed the lawyer, because the lawyer was unable to show that dealing with that particular aspect was not their responsibility.

Tax aspects of a case have often been the culprit. Firms should have very detailed carve-out clauses limiting and clarifying what they are doing – and not doing – for the client.

The second reason is financial. If you set out what work is included in the (high) core price and what isn't, everyone has clarity. "Mission creep" (doing more and more work within the initial price) is avoided, as is a plea for a higher fee or even a surprise bill at the end of the case and, therefore, client unhappiness.

The client should be told what you are doing, what the price is, and that any extra work will mean an extra fee, as you don't undertake *any* legal work without charging for it.

Of course, the lawyer then has to be rigorous in looking out for "mission creep" and raising this with the client as soon as it arises.

Some lawyers I see are superb at this – raising "mission creep" immediately and securing further payment for further work. Don't be afraid of doing this. Clients are not repelled by it at all. They wouldn't supply further produce to their customers for free, say, and they don't expect you to. Give them an inch, though…

Rule 4 – Clients have to pay you and pay you quickly

- It's not a lawyer's job to just do law

- It's not a lawyer's job to do law and send out bills

- It is a lawyer's job to do law, send out bills, *and to get those bills paid quickly*

An unpaid bill doesn't just deprive your firm of the cash it needs to pay your salary, to pay all the overheads around you, and to enable the firm to reward its people with pay rises… it's much worse than that:

- Until your bill is paid, depending on the jurisdiction you operate in, the firm may have to find the cash to pay the VAT or other sales tax that attaches to your bill as soon as it is raised. In England, for example, the firm has to find 20% of the bill *out of its own pocket* to pay the VAT that was on the bill, and

- Assuming your firm is profitable, income tax or corporation tax will have to be paid by the firm *out of its own pocket* on the amount you have billed.

When they are first raised, therefore, your bills are *a setback* for the firm. A big-billing lawyer is far from being a perfect lawyer. They could be a perfect disaster.

The bigger the unpaid bill or bills, the bigger the problem you have caused your firm. Whoever thought that bills could be a problem? But they are, until they are paid.

If a law firm suffers from, and tolerates, a culture where *billing* is the emphasis rather than *cash*, then the faster the law firm grows, the faster and the greater it will suffer.

If you were the owner of a law firm, what would you think of one of your lawyers who was working hard but who was, in fact, bringing the firm to its knees by using up all your cash? Would you think they were perfect?

Too many lawyers are obsessed with how good their legal work is, and/or are obsessed with how much they are billing. There is only one obsession that counts, and that's an obsession with *how much cash they've brought in.*

So, as well as having "Pride in Pricing", Perfect Lawyers at The Perfect Legal Business have a "Cash Commitment".

To me, control over the credit that is extended to a client (whether that be in terms of unbilled WIP or unbilled disbursements or unpaid bills) is *the lawyer's* responsibility, not something that is outsourced (for example) to Credit Control. Lawyers looking to

Business Support to clear up their mess is not a good look.

It cannot be right that a lawyer can behave in a totally cavalier and "un-cash" way and then look to someone else to clear up their mess whilst they get promoted and rewarded for having high billings.

Obviously, there are various work-types (Legal Aid work, or Personal Injury or Clinical Negligence work, for example) where all that I say here does not apply, but the route to fast payment with privately-paying work begins at the very start of the journey with a client.

The rule about you needing to be paid quickly should not be on page 8 of a standard "client care" letter. It should be part of the open discussion between lawyer and client at the outset.

The safest way to ensure fast payment is, of course, to get money on account. If a client refuses to pay that, why are they refusing? What is that telling you – that they can't pay? That they won't pay?

Neither is attractive in a client. That should raise alarm bells. And if you do have to extend credit, why offer individual clients more than 7 days' credit?

If a business client doesn't pay after, say, 30 days, put them on "stop". Let them know from the beginning that you – like them – are a cash business.

Summary of client selection and engagement

Having set these four rules in respect of new clients – in addition to all AML, etc., requirements that you have in place – you can be more confident that clients who do satisfy your rules and who are thus allowed to come on board, will be good for you personally and for your firm as a whole – in the longer term as well as in the shorter term.

Your ability to properly look after these good clients will not be undermined by you playing a "numbers" game, based on the misguided view that the more clients you have, the better.

Like the rules enforced by bouncers at popular nightclubs, there should be a strict code as to which clients can actually come in (and who can *stay* in – there should always be a readiness to sack clients who fall foul of the rules).

In the shape of its Perfect Lawyers, The Perfect Legal Business sets these very clear rules and thus rebalances power between the law firm and client in the correct way.

Some clients might be repelled at that stage, but The Perfect Legal Business and its lawyers can and should have the confidence that those clients are no loss to the business.

In line with the general thread that runs through this book, by which we want *to do less, better, for more*, this all means you will have fewer clients, who are better clients, and whom you can look after more and bill more – and no one will be happier than the client.

But clients are one thing – their case is another thing altogether. Even where the client gets over all your bars, let's not forget that every case that is taken on by any lawyer could be dynamite – in more ways than one.

CHAPTER 6

THERE ARE CLIENTS – AND THERE ARE CASES

If you said to an investor (such as an aspiring Equity Partner in a law firm – they're investors), "Look, you really should buy into this law firm at a cost of hundreds of thousands of pounds, *though we can't be sure that the business will even be here next year*", what would they do?

Correct.

Unbelievably, this is how it is with law firms, certainly in England. On paper, they are literally year-to-year businesses. And the reason for this is Professional Indemnity Insurance.

Professional Indemnity Insurance here lasts 12 months at a time – 18 months at the most. And when it comes to renewal each year, if no one will insure your firm because you have a terrible claims record, it's simply a case of "no insurance, no lights on".

And whilst it's easy to think your firm could never rack up a dangerous claims record on the "bread and butter" types of work that you do, I can tell you that if you haven't had the pleasure of dealing with the claims and

PII impact of a poor lawyer doing everyday work, you haven't lived.

So, having Risk Management as an obsession is another part of The Perfect Legal Business and should be part of the make-up of the Perfect Lawyer. Individual lawyers should be fussy about what *cases* they take on, as well as what clients they take on. The bigger the fee, the more wary you should be. Not all that glitters is gold.

One of the "golden rules" I mentioned above that every lawyer should lay down when taking any client on is – don't dabble. And I mentioned the other golden rule – "define the retainer". You should set out in writing at the outset what you are doing *and what you are NOT* doing. It's an amazing feeling when you can point to a letter that says your firm wasn't dealing with the aspect that has just exploded.

There should be a set of rules that apply across each team and across the firm to *cases* that you can take on, as well as those that apply to clients that you take on. These rules could relate to the size of the case (and thus the size of any resulting claim), the nature of the legal expertise required (is it something that you are genuinely good at?) and the urgency of the case (is there a limitation date next week or month?). If a client wants to move an ongoing case to you from another law firm, that should raise alarm bells.

It's far better to lose fees than to lose your shirt.

Of course, firms should be fussy about what *lawyers* they take on, too, and what lawyers they keep on. They need to be obsessed with quality control, supervision, and training – don't just pay lip service to these things. Having no lawyer is better than having a bad lawyer!

Do Team Leaders really know what quality of work their lawyers are churning out? Or are Team Leaders weighed down with huge caseloads that mean they can't really manage and lead their teams?

In a world where emails, texts, and WhatsApp messages can't be supervised like "the post" could be in the old days, who knows what's coming into or going out of a law firm?

Firms, through their Team Leaders, need to look under the bonnet. Don't be satisfied with a tick-box exercise in relation to file reviews just before the Lexcel inspector or some other assessor arrives.

A particular risk arises when a law firm tries to branch out into new areas of law – areas where they have no expertise, so no ability to monitor quality or risk in the work being done by their new lawyers.

Perfect Lawyers *want* their work to be examined and sanity-checked – whatever level they are at. It's a team game, and ploughing on without ever having a second pair of expert eyes on a case is unwise.

And lawyers need to comply with the firm's rules. A feature of a dangerous lawyer is one who ignores internal (and external) rules.

Law firms are full of Business Support teams who run round after imperfect lawyers, tidying up after them.

CHAPTER 7

PERFECT LAWYERS AND "MONEY"

Assuming a lawyer remains wary of clients at all times, and that they raise the bar when it comes to taking on new clients and cases, and they adhere to all internal and external rules, we can now move on to look at the lawyers as they carry out their work on those cases for those clients – not just as lawyers, but as essential (indeed, the *only*) generators of revenue in what is, after all, a business. And a business with acute pressure on it to generate cash and to grow every year.

So that you can see what the input from a lawyer needs to be, I discuss in this section how the business and finances of a law firm work. I hope this is helpful not just in framing and guiding a lawyer's ways of working going forward, but in arming a lawyer for their future careers as managers and leaders within a law firm, or as owners of a law firm, or as investors in a law firm. I wish I'd had this kind of detailed education before I'd set sail.

Generally, we need a lawyer to maximise and grow revenue (as I define it here) but not to undermine their profitability by having debtors, claims, or taking up the time of Management or Business Support who have to clear up around them. We need a lawyer who is financially efficient and effective – in profit and, more importantly, cash terms.

And the business needs more than a static, plateau kind of contribution from its lawyers here. It's not enough for the business if the lawyers bill the same each year. The cost of everything goes up every year. To even stand still, law firms have to *grow* profit and cash.

And the lawyers need that growth, too. How can they expect pay rises year after year if their contribution to the business hasn't increased? The question, therefore, is how do lawyers achieve that growth?

I believe that lawyers can achieve this by their own direct efforts. This growth is vital not just because it generates so much profit and cash quite easily, but also because it is the prelude to – and the launch pad for – wider growth later, which is achieved by lawyers and their law firms working together.

There is an ongoing discussion in our marketplace about whether billing by the hour is dead, and there are some vocal and influential supporters of what is called "value billing". The former means time is a limiting factor on what you can bill, and the latter means you can break free of that restricting factor.

I really like the sound of "value billing". I think clients do, too – when the outcome for them is a low fee for a complicated but low-value job. I don't think they like the idea as much when it is a high-value but quick job.

From what I see across the country and the world, law firms and clients are still wedded to the hourly rate and to time-charge billing. It is here to stay for the foreseeable future, believe me (though it has never played a part in the work of some teams who have long been quoting fixed fees).

As the "chargeable hour" is still prevalent in many areas of law, growth can come from the existing lawyers recording more of the hours that they do, and by new lawyers doing and recording good hours, and by all these lawyers billing more of the hours that have been recorded. Growth is also achieved by applying an hourly rate that reflects a pride in pricing and which is commensurate with the seniority of the work that is being done.

If the lawyer is already working hard (and they usually are), then the first thing any lawyer needs to do is make sure that maximum chargeable hours are not only being *done* (and not just by them, but in a good team structure where all vessels are full), but also that every minute spent on files is being *captured*. Every captured minute then needs to be billed, and the bills need to be paid quickly, so that all of this hard work translates into profit and cash – and soon.

This kind of growth is a huge opportunity at every firm that I see. The first phase of "growth", therefore, usually doesn't need more cases.

The need for growth in a law firm

A trait that separates "Perfect Legal Business" law firms from those that are not, is a desire for "growth".

"Growth", to me, is an over-arching oxygen that moves a law firm in the right direction. "Growth", of course, has a very particular and central place in the legal industry. It is our opium. In the PR, marketing, and legal recruitment markets, you could be forgiven for feeling like you are failing if you aren't "growing" aggressively and noisily.

I am a believer that any business has to "grow" to stay strong. "Growth", though, is absolutely vital in a law firm, as I hope to demonstrate here. But growth in what?

Yes, growth in client numbers, growth in the "noise" that a firm creates, growth in profile, growth in turnover, growth in the number of offices, growth in the number of Partners, growth in the number of work-types offered, growth in the number of lawyers named in the directories as "leaders", growth in awards won, and growth in staff numbers, can all have a positive effect.

These are the things that are universally recognised in our industry as the badges of a successful law firm. They are all the stuff of press releases, awards submissions, and staff conferences. They attract talent. They create profile and "noise".

I had growth in all of these areas – and a lot of it. It is some achievement for your law firm to be "the fastest-growing law firm in the UK" out of 10,000 or so law firms, but that's what my firm was.

I would literally never aim for that again. It nearly killed me and it nearly killed us, because there are some other key "growth" dimensions that need to be added to the above list.

If the things I listed above are the *only* growth indicators that a firm pursues or measures or indeed realises, these apparent "successes" can actually generate unwelcome pressure on a firm, to put it mildly.

The reason is that the areas of growth I listed can all too easily go hand in hand with other, less welcome and less palatable forms of "growth. Growth in debtors, growth in your overdraft, growth in borrowings more widely than just from your bank, and growth in the Business Support overhead, for example, as more and more people run faster and faster to try to keep up with the constant inflow of new people and with constant change.

If you were starting a new law firm from scratch, it would be easy to set a course for rapid growth so that these dangers and risks are avoided. However, the reality of seeking growth is very different in a large and long-established legal business with complex inter-personnel and personal relationships and a history of doing things in a certain way. These may be firms where the wrong things are rewarded, varied behaviours between lawyers get accommodated, and where lawyers do things in their own idiosyncratic ways, involving various workarounds.

An established law firm is full to the brim of challenges to growth, and there are countless obstacles in the way of a firm that is trying to bring and accelerate the right sort of growth.

Challenges to growth in a law firm

Consider the following list of challenges – which are all real. In fact, the list could be much longer.

- Owners are often of different ages and, therefore, have different things motivating them

- Managing Partners often have heavy caseloads

- Team Leaders can have heavy caseloads

- Lawyers' caseloads are too high, so files are in storage

- The partnership model doesn't always bring "fleetness of foot" in terms of decision-making

- Absent other differentiators, a firm often has no choice but to compete on price

- There is often no real quality control over the legal work that is carried out

- Lawyers in some teams sometimes don't trust lawyers in other teams

- Lawyers can be capable of nodding as though they mean "yes", but they then continue just as they did before; they do not always do what the firm needs them to do

- "Billing" is usually the prime KPI – low pricing, low chargeable hours, and high write-offs are all overlooked – as are debtors

- Some work is, by definition, "in production" for an awfully long time before it generates cash

- Some work requires law firms to fund high levels of disbursements or marketing fees

- Everyone can deliver their service (or not deliver their service) in the way that they choose

- The lawyers can price the work as they wish

- The lawyers can bill the work as they wish – and can discount WIP

- Partners might not be leading by example

- There is often a push for every team to market only itself

- There is no real concern over the profitability of clients

- There is no pressure on teams or Team Leaders to grow the right things

- Compliance with policies is effectively optional – and Partners can be the worst

- A firm can have too many clients – it can't begin to understand and develop them

- Clients are seen just as cases, owned by the lawyer dealing with the case

- Lawyers talk about "my client" instead of "our client"

- The client journey is often short-lived because service is no better than "average"

- Clients are never asked how the firm is doing during the case

- There is no visibility over where profit is being made, and whether other factors are undermining that profit

- Cash is always tight, so there is no investment

- Pay might be behind that of competitor firms

- There might be no clear career path for star performers

- The way forward is often seen as "More marketing!" to win new clients (on price) – who then go into storage

- The Marketing team have no ammunition to set the firm apart from competitors

- The firm tries to *sell* things to clients – not to extend care proactively

The list could go on. It's hard to grow a law firm, isn't it? How on earth do you achieve the desired and vital growth in the face of even a small number of these challenges, let alone all of them?

The short answer is that you need your lawyers to change direction, to travel down a new road at an increasing speed, and to do so as a team. Whatever challenges a firm faces, a firm's lawyers can secure the right growth and thus change the firm's destiny, or they can totally hold the firm back.

A law firm is always on a spiral up, or on a spiral down. There is no plateau of rest. Its lawyers dictate which spiral it is on.

It is for the law firm to create the right environment in which the lawyers want to change and do change.

Real dangers await the law firm that doesn't achieve constant growth – growth, that is, of the right sort.

And to achieve that growth, let's look (by better understanding how a law firm's finances work) at the growth that is needed and at what The Perfect Legal Business needs of its lawyers.

CHAPTER 8

GROWTH IN WHAT?

All the growth types mentioned above can be growth of the right sort, PROVIDED ALWAYS (forgive the lawyer speak) that those forms of growth are accompanied by growth in some key *additional* areas. That is, in some hard *business* areas.

Ah, you mean we need growth in "profits"?

(Let me apologise at this point if I am teaching you to suck eggs. I have, however, seen more than enough people in law firms at even middle- and senior-Management levels who do not fully grasp the basics I set out here. It took a baptism of fire and years of sleepless nights for me to truly learn about these things.)

No. I don't just mean we need to see growth in "profits". As a first step, we need to understand the fundamental principle that in a law firm, we need to look at two things – "profit" and "cash". Both are vital. They are completely separate and different things.

Not everyone understands that "profit" and "cash" are hugely different and separate things in any business but particularly in law firms. Treating them as the same thing can be fatal.

When running a law firm, you need to look at your business in PROFIT terms and then, completely separately, look at it in CASH terms.

As I will show, you can get wildly different pictures from each of these examinations as to how the business is doing.

In a nutshell:

- Lack of profit is painful.

- Lack of cash is fatal.

Firms can watch their profit and think they are doing okay or that they have got time to improve it. All the while, there could be a cash bomb going off at any moment that will bring things to a juddering halt.

Many businesses that fail are "profitable", they just took their eyes off the "cash" ball.

You have to understand and watch both. Both can lead to the death of the law firm. The only differences are that profit decline is often visible and slow, and cash decline is often hidden but sudden.

- A decline in profit doesn't always kill a business

- Having no cash *always* kills a business.

A good friend of mine in the legal sector once explained all of this to a law firm Managing Partner, whose reply was, "Bloody hell – when did they change all that?"

Profit

Let's look at "profit" first.

For there to be a profit in a law firm, there needs to be more "revenue" than "expenditure". Simple, you would have thought.

In a law firm, however, the waters around this simple concept are muddy and misleading.

For in a law firm, "revenue" comes in *two* guises. You don't have any choice about that. It's the law. *Both ways can fool you completely. Either can be completely illusory.*

(Interestingly, as of 2025 in the UK and elsewhere, "revenue" – when it comes to law firms – includes a very substantial 'new kid on the block', namely interest earned from your bank on client monies held on deposit by the firm. At current interest rates, this is generating game-changing numbers for law firms. In some cases, it is keeping the lights on. Rates are already declining. In this book, I ignore this source of revenue completely. We are law firms who should earn revenue by selling legal services. We are not banks.)

Let's look at the two usual types of revenue so we can identify *precisely* the type of revenue a law firm needs its lawyers to generate:

(a) Revenue resulting from bills you raise on your files

In the simplest of terms, if your firm bills £100 plus VAT (or some other sales tax, depending on where you operate) in a year and you pay staff and suppliers £60, then you have revenues of £100, you have to pay VAT of £20 to the Government, and you have made "profit" of £40. Easy.

But what if those £100 (plus VAT) bills haven't been paid yet?

Well, you have still made a £40 profit in the eyes of the law.

But you've got to pay the staff and suppliers £60 out of your own money, and in this example you have to use a further £20 of your *own* cash to pay the VAT.

So, even before your clients have paid you, you are paying out money in respect of the lawyers' salaries and overheads *and* you are paying the £20 VAT. (That £20 may not sound like a lot, but in a firm in, say, England with unpaid bills of, say, £250,000 – and there are a lot of them – that is VAT of £50,000 that has to be found, depending on timings).

Worse still, as these bills form part of your revenue and profit, you have to pay *tax* on that profit. Again, out of your own money if you leave these bills unpaid.

That business is doomed. "But we've made a profit!" it screams.

It will die a profitable business. As I said above, many businesses that die are indeed *profitable* – cash (or lack of it) is a separate thing.

In my firm, as with many other firms, we were very busy working on client files and sending lots of bills out to clients. We were, therefore, very *profitable*. We rejoiced. But our lack of focus on the "cash" side meant we had a growing "Debtors" book. By giving our expertise to clients and letting them keep the cash that was rightly ours for too long, we were funding our clients' businesses rather than our own.

And, in our case, we were having to borrow money to pay the VAT.

It's insanity. Firms that do this are an expensive lender's dream.

We were grinding away, watching our cash deplete, paying handsomely to use someone else's cash to run the business (i.e., the Bank's cash), with panic and pressure setting in whilst – on the face of it – we were "doing well". *Success that doesn't involve cash will kill you.*

A surefire way of hurting a law firm, therefore, is to have lots of lawyers who are busy, who are getting paid good salaries, who send out lots of bills, and who then don't get those bills paid quickly.

This first type of profit (i.e., profit based on "revenue" in the form of bills you have sent out) will therefore go up, and on paper, you'll be doing well. But cash will be pouring out of the business in terms of salaries, overheads, and VAT, and then in the shape of tax on your "profit".

Your very growth in profit will do you in, in the end.

This "disease" (trading and growing without the necessary cash coming in) has actually got a name. The business world calls it "overtrading" – Google it – but I prefer to call it being blinded by empty success, and getting drunk on vanity, because there's too much hot air and frantic activity going on around the firm that all makes you think you're great.

The first thing I now do when I start a "growth" project with a law firm is to ask to see their Debtors ledger. If their "way" is to focus on "billings", and they live with an Aged Debtors book which has columns headed 0-30 days, 30-60 days, 60-90 days, 90-120 days, and yes, 120+ days, I immediately shift my focus.

Any increase in their marketing or growth in their lawyer numbers, Partner numbers, teams, offices, billing, and clients, will do them harm, not good.

(b) The second type of "revenue" – thin air

It gets worse. I said that a law firm (whether it likes it or not) makes a profit from two types of "revenue". The first type of revenue is "bills sent out". The second type of "revenue" that goes towards a firm's profit is even more dangerous than the first.

In most law firms, there will be a lot of work done by lawyers who have recorded lots of time "on the system" – time that will hopefully be billed later.

Under UK laws, a law firm has to value that Work in Progress, or WIP, on the first day of every financial year, to arrive at what is called the "Opening Value". Then, it has to be valued again on the last day of every financial year to arrive at the "Closing Value".

If the Closing Value is higher than the Opening Value, the difference (called the WIP *Uplift*) counts as the second type of "revenue", and it has to be added to your "profit" for that year.

Sounds good? "Hey, fantastic – we haven't even billed that work and our profit's gone up! We're rich!" How good is that? Thin air gets added to a firm's profit.

Actually, it's not good at all. It's a nightmare.

This "thin air" revenue (and therefore profit), like the first type of revenue and profit (which was based on bills sent out but not yet paid), also gets taxed. You thus have to pay tax (that is, pay tax *in cash*) on this profit too – but you haven't even billed the client yet, let alone been paid by them. So, guess whose money is going to be used to pay that tax? Correct – the firm's. This "profit", therefore, is again not something to get excited about – it is yet another drain on a firm's limited bucket of cash.

As you can see, there are two types of profit, but neither is necessarily the only stuff that counts – cash.

You can maybe see more clearly now why a lawyer should keep their WIP at a minimum (by billing it regularly – and getting those bills paid) and why writing off dead WIP and accurately valuing any "live" WIP at year-end are all vital to arriving at an accurate picture of a law firm's finances.

To conclude this section – the revenue and profit that a firm actually wants (and which it needs to grow every year) can be very clearly articulated:

A law firm needs billing-based profit, not WIP-based profit, but where those bills are paid quickly.

You can thus see what makes a lawyer perfect or imperfect from a law firm's perspective.

Let me dwell a little longer on a point I have just made. The bills really do need to be paid quickly. Let's talk more about *cash*. You and your law firm will be all the better for it.

CHAPTER 9

CASH

In the same way, and to exactly the same degree, that a human needs oxygen, a business needs cash. Cash, not just profit. They are different things. Profit is no substitute for oxygen.

And a law firm needs an awful lot of cash. Every month. That cash can only come from its lawyers.

Running a law firm can easily become no more than an exercise in counting "cash in" and "cash out" on a daily, let alone weekly or monthly basis.

The monthly salary bill in a law firm, for example, is completely out of kilter when set against other non-law businesses with a similar headcount. Indeed, "payday" on the 28th (or whatever day of the month it is when salaries go out) is usually the moment when law firms that die, die.

Law firms have a voracious appetite for cash, each and every month. It never stops. And if you try to grow a law firm by bringing in new lawyers or teams or offices, from Month #1 of any such enterprise, your cash appetite goes through the roof (whilst it may take you until, say, Month #6 before those lawyers start bringing in any cash).

A firm can roughly work out what its monthly break-even *cash* figure is – how much cash is going to go out. That dictates how much cash it needs coming in each month, which in most firms is very different to how much it needs to do in billing each month, of course. "Bills out" can be very different to "cash in". Indeed, where there is VAT or another sales tax, "Bills out" can actually mean "more cash out" when you factor in the VAT impact of unpaid bills that we looked at in the last chapter.

Such is the ocean of cash that flows out of law firms that a couple of difficult trading months would bring real anguish for many law firms.

The problem with cash is that any business only has a limited amount of the stuff. Most law firms are small or medium-sized enterprises. They are typically owner-managed businesses. I believe that both internally and externally, people often think law firms have a bottomless pit of money. It's so not like that.

The cash that most law firms have access to is usually limited to the cash that the owners have put into or left in the business on the one hand, and money that the bank lets it use by way of an overdraft (at a high cost), on the other.

From the perspective of your law firm's owners, what kind of lawyer are you:

- The Perfect Lawyer – doing lots of work, recording all the time, billing it all as soon as you can, and getting paid quickly? or

- The imperfect lawyer – not catching all the time spent, not billing it when it can be billed, not billing it all even when you do bill it, and doing bills which don't get paid, so the firm has to find the additional cash to pay the VAT on unpaid bills and to pay the tax on the billing you have done, as well as paying your salary and all the firm's overheads out of its own pocket?

All the forms of growth that I mentioned above are fine, but they are, in fact, dangerous if they are not accompanied on the "growth" bus by a growth in cash reserves (which flows from a growth in profit of the right type; namely, profit based on paid bills).

This is all the more important when we remind ourselves that The Perfect Legal Business is made up of great people – great Partners, great lawyers, and a Business Support team at the top of its game.

There's a lot more to it than money, of course, but great people usually want great salaries – and expect *growing* salaries – as a reward for ongoing loyalty and hard work.

Great people don't take "standing still" in reward terms too well, particularly when their marketplaces are buoyant, and there always seem to be competitor law firms out there with fat chequebooks.

The business, therefore, needs to generate more and more profit and cash to meet those salary demands, and that depends on the lawyers, well, generating more and more profit and cash.

This may all sound hard-nosed, and you may be thinking "So, it's all about the money, is it?" Yes. It absolutely is. But let's embrace that rather than run away from it.

I've been in law firms that had a lot of money, and in law firms that have not had a lot of money. I know where I'd rather be, and I know where the people were happier.

I am – now – *all* about the money, but as you will see in this book, I am also passionate about there being another side to the coin (if you excuse the pun).

So, the first steps down the road towards becoming The Perfect Legal Business are for a law firm to recognise that it is all about GROWTH IN CASH, and for the lawyers in the firm to embrace this pillar of business, too, and to act on it. 'No cash' means fewer rewards and limited opportunities.

To repeat what I said earlier – the necessary cash can only come from the firm's lawyers. It is not "someone else's" problem.

If a law firm does not achieve growth each year in profit and – more importantly – growth in cash, then one inevitable impact, because there is always only a limited supply of cash, is that it has to control its costs (including salaries) going forward.

And those costs don't even stay the same every year. There seems to be universal upward pressure on salaries and on suppliers' prices – whether that be paper, Professional Indemnity Insurance, rent, IT costs, etc., even when we aren't talking about major investments or upgrades.

So, *to even stand still*, a law firm has to grow every year in both profit *and cash* terms. Great people are vulnerable if they don't believe they are in the right place to enjoy increasing rewards (i.e., pay rises, and wider investment in them and their development) year after year. You can see that there has to be constant profit and cash growth if the firm is to remain on a healthy, forward-only trajectory.

Lawyers cannot, in my view, expect salary and reward increases if their contribution to the business is not increasing each year. That would take the firm closer to the cliff – and eventually over it.

Standing still (in profit and cash terms) is a suicide note for a law firm, and not a very long suicide note, at that.

The fact that your profit looks good means nothing. It could be based on unpaid bills and/or on WIP uplift, rather than on bills that have been turned into cash. "Profit" can be dangerously misleading. Your billing could be high, but so could your debtors, and so could your WIP.

These other things can make you relax because "profit" looks good, rather than making you drive growth in "profit based on paid bills". It is easy to be comforted by profit figures that, on the face of it, give reasons to be cheerful.

To demonstrate this, instead of talking about a whole law firm, let's take a high-billing, high-performing, growing, "profitable" *team within a law firm.* That "fantastic" team could, in fact, be hurting you.

Hard to believe? It's true. To work out whether that team is an asset to the business, or a problem for it, it's not enough to look at how busy they are, or at their marketing activity, their awards, their billing, or even at their "profit". As we saw above, you can easily make profitability look good – just send out lots of bills.

You need to look at the team's *cash impact*.

We designed and used something that I called a Team Cash Impact Statement, which looked at the overall impact of a team on the *cash* (i.e., on the oxygen or actual health) of the business.

We need to lift the bonnet and look beyond a team's "big billing" or "big profit" headlines. This tool was a very helpful but very sobering instrument. A team's Cash Impact Statement looked like this:

Aspect	Year-to-Date Cash Position +/- (£)
Billings	
Less unpaid bills	
Less the VAT or sales tax the firm has had to pay on their unpaid bills	
Less disbursements paid out and not yet recovered	
Less disbursements written off	
Less salaries, PAYE, NI, pensions, etc.	
Less team marketing spend	
Less practising certificates, training, etc.	

Aspect	Year-to-Date Cash Position +/- (£)
Team's net cash impact	

At the time, I was leading what was perceived by everyone to be "a highly successful law firm". It felt, however, like really hard work. Much harder than it should have been. Why weren't we having a glorious time? I needed to know why that was. The reason was simply cash. Using this tool, I could look at a team and see the degree to which they were truly helping or hindering our business at any point in our financial year, regardless of how they were doing in illusory "billing" or "profit" terms.

A team may be "profitable" but may, at the same time, be really holding your business back by draining it of cash.

I was able to show at the end of Month #9, for example, that one *huge and hugely 'profitable'* team of lawyers had, overall, brought in less *cash* to the firm than one part-time lawyer in another area of work! That was a total eye-opener.

This all underlines the area that a law firm needs its lawyers to focus on – it's *always* about cash generation and cash collection. Start running without breathing, without oxygen, and see how far you get.

It also, of course, underlines what – in the eyes of *a law firm* – the Perfect Lawyer looks like.

If you've ever spent time in a personal or business capacity with businesses "out there" – i.e., with non-lawyers – you will quickly see that they have no time for anything other than cash. They aren't fooled by "billings" or by an increase in orders coming in or by more goods being sent out.

"Cash" is the major part of the architecture of non-law businesses.

Let's reflect on how various business models around us behave in "cash" terms. This will help us to see just how important "cash positivity" is seen by normal businesses, as opposed to law firms' "cash negativity", plus what disciplines a firm needs its lawyers to focus on (if their work-types permit it) so that it moves in the right direction in cash terms.

Some work-types do not permit cash positivity. A law firm needs to have deep pockets if that's the only work it does, or it needs to have quick-burn work to balance things out and to fund the long-burn work.

What follows here will demonstrate how normal businesses are obsessed with where they are on a cash spectrum, and it will indicate that a lot of law firms are totally at the wrong end of that spectrum. This is bizarre as law firms actually need *more* cash than most businesses due to their mammoth monthly salary bills.

Looking at the cash personality of businesses, at one extreme you have businesses such as insurance companies that take your cash and might *never* give you anything in return. They also invest that cash to try to make further profit out of it. That's *cash-positive*!

Then, there are businesses that, for example, sell gift vouchers or Christmas hampers – they do give you something in return for your cash, but only a long time later. That's *cash-positive*, too.

Then you have the Amazon model, where they also get your cash before they've given you anything. Typically, having got your cash up front, businesses like this demand long credit terms from the people they have to pay – their suppliers. They can thus retain a fortune in cash in this way for a long time. Again, *cash-positive*.

Then, moving across the spectrum, you have the "bricks and mortar" retail model, where you hand over your cash in a shop at the same time as you get what you are buying. The shop gets your cash immediately. If the retailer has buying power, it will demand that its suppliers give it anything up to 120 days' credit – so they have time to sell the goods *and* be sat on a cash pile for a long time. Again, *cash-positive*.

Delaying the day that they have to pay for the things they've been paid for, is an art form. Businesses try to get their suppliers to fund their businesses, whereas law firms regularly fund their clients' businesses. Businesses out there wage a constant cash battle, trying to make sure that the credit period they give their customers is short and that the credit periods they get from their suppliers are long. As a profession, we just aren't bothered enough about all of this.

All of the above businesses are clear cash businesses. No cash? No supply. There is no cash at risk at all for them. Assuming they get the sales, they are strong businesses in cash terms because they have made themselves *cash-positive*. McDonalds doesn't have any bad debts. It has a cash mountain. It gets your money, and it pays its suppliers months later.

Having a "cash strategy" was a central part of the planning when these businesses were set up. It had to be, or they would never have been able to grow. They "wargame" the cash position and put methods in place to keep them as cash-positive as possible. They would otherwise run out of cash.

In the legal profession, we generally don't pay the cash profile of the business a blind bit of notice. We now come to where, on the cash spectrum, you'll find most law firms.

The opposite of a healthy cash-positive state is to be *cash-negative* – where you use *your own* cash to fund and effect the supply to the customer, and then you have to try to recover payment from your client or customer later. It's a very different ball game. Cash negativity brings cash pain.

Such businesses move away from being brutal cash businesses in the Amazon or McDonalds mould because they supply their goods or services *before* they are paid. Law firms typically fall into this bracket. They supply their expensively-produced advice (advice produced by cash-hungry lawyers) long before they get paid for it.

It is a real question of trust here. I know that some work-types (personal injury, clinical negligence, conveyancing, all Legal Aid work, etc.) don't have "debtor" dangers, but across our profession, lawyers very often supply their services on a buy now, pay later basis – that is, *on credit*.

Lawyers usually set out the time for payment somewhere in a long retainer letter, and after the services are supplied, they send the client an invoice.

An invoice is effectively a begging letter that, hopefully the client will pay on time. Of course, clients don't all do that.

So, many law firms are *credit* businesses rather than *cash* businesses. But even within "credit" businesses, there is another spectrum.

At one extreme of this other spectrum, you have a wide array of non-legal businesses – designers, printers, IT companies, stationery and office equipment companies, and so on.

Typically, these businesses might not have the deepest of pockets and may not have been treated well by their banks over the years, so they won't have big overdraft facilities they can dip into. This means that they are very good at getting the cash in if their invoices aren't paid on time.

They immediately put you on "stop" and/or they demand cash for any further deliveries, and/or they pass the case to their debt recovery companies who get to work on it – they simply can't afford not to.

At the other extreme of this spectrum of credit businesses, you have law firms. *We are all too often at the wrong end of the wrong spectrum.*

You would not see many of the non-legal businesses just mentioned with a "Debtors" list that had so many columns on it – 0-30 days, 30-60 days, 60-90 days, 90-120 days. Columns showing (huge) unpaid bills that are

120+ or even 180+ days old are a regular sight at law firms.

I sit down and talk with Credit Control teams. They want to be let loose for the good of the business, but they are constantly prevented from chasing "good clients" by the lawyers...

The "normal" businesses above would be horrified and completely perplexed that a business (particularly one with a staggering cash appetite like that of a law firm) could allow so much of its cash to remain in its customers' pockets. What on earth could it be using, in terms of cash, to run the firm? The answer is often an overdraft. It borrows money to make up for its woeful cash behaviours.

When I was Managing Partner, I did not have my eye firmly enough on the "unpaid bills" ball. And, of course, even though many bills were not being paid on time, as well as paying all the lawyers' salaries and all the overheads, we were using our own money to pay the VAT on the bills that hadn't been paid. That became too great a drain on our limited cash resource, so we started borrowing money to pay the VAT.

And we were paying tax on the huge profits that the as-yet-unpaid bills had generated. By borrowing that money, too.

In a booming business – don't forget, we were the UK's fastest-growing law firm! – it constantly felt like the walls were closing in. This was overtrading, par excellence.

Whilst we had done noble work that we could be proud of in relation to service levels and in terms of proactive care (that is, work that favoured the *client*), I had not had the same focus on making our law firm and our lawyers more cash-focused, all of which would have favoured our business.

Frankly, I didn't know then what I know now. I didn't know what the options were, other than barking at everyone about getting money on account and setting up a robust and determined credit control system.

I didn't realise that we could undergo a cultural shift towards becoming more of a cash business. Instead of engendering and nurturing a cultural shift, I relied on, well, as I say, barking. We had lots of regular chasing of clients and lawyers by a brilliant Credit Controller. And other resources got sucked into fighting this fight, too – our amazing Office Head spent her time on this instead of working her magic and spreading gold dust over our people in other areas of the business.

It doesn't have to be that way, as the song goes. In The Perfect Legal Business, it is not like that at all. *The Perfect Legal Business – courtesy of its Perfect Lawyers – is far more of a cash business than a typical law firm is.*

As we discussed above, instead of the payment terms being lost in a long retainer letter, the time for payment is made very clear to clients by the lawyers at the outset. It's the lawyers' job to get cash in, and it's therefore part of the lawyers' opening discussion: "We obviously can't work with clients who don't pay on time". Easy. Are you really going to take on a client who says in response, "Hey – wait a minute – that's not fair – I'm not happy with that at all"?

Where your branding is clear and your differentiators are strong, where your lawyers' "Pride in Pricing" and

"Cash Commitment" are high, lawyers should feel perfectly fine in setting a high price, setting out narrow retainers, insisting on quick payment, insisting on cash on account, and in dealing with any late payers themselves rather than seeing them as someone else's problem – particularly if all of these things are part of the ongoing performance review and part of the lawyers' career development programme. The Perfect Legal Business thus moves, courtesy of its Perfect Lawyers, from being a credit-ravaged business to being more of a cash business.

Any business that delivers its goods or services without a clear cash plan, and without a short timeline between supply and payment, will feel pain. I know.

Even where a team is in a "steady" phase, without any significant recruitment going on, the "cash" challenge is a real one. But step out of the "steady" phase into any kind of "growth" phase, and watch what happens. As soon as you add new recruits to a team, the cash outflow increases. That month. And yes, hopefully the new lawyers will do some bills quite soon – but absent fast billing and fast payment of those bills, they add to the problem. The star new lawyer who has billed £100k in their first 6 months? Have those bills been paid?

These are all aspects to be borne in mind when growth is pursued when a law firm recruits lawyers from other firms. As a route to growth, it is not always a road paved with gold and is often a road paved with pain.

We can thus see a key feature of the Perfect Legal Business and of Perfect Lawyers. They have in their DNA a hunger not just for profit but for *cash* – and for cash *growth*.

The hunger is a focused and constant hunger. Without growth each year in profit *and cash*, a cash-hungry business like a law firm begins to become short of breath – panting and wheezing and slowing down, instead of stampeding down the pitch.

And who can a firm look to, to achieve these things? The lawyers who work there – that's who. There is literally no one else.

Finally, here, while I say the Perfect Legal Business puts cash "front of house", and it sets out at the start of every financial year to achieve increased profit and cash reserves by the end of the year, there are *two* sides to this coin.

I believe that it's perfectly in order and absolutely nothing to be ashamed of to charge a high price for your legal services, and to bill for every minute your lawyers spend on a file, and to insist on quick payment of bills, *provided* you are discharging the role that I believe law firms and solicitors have in society. That is, to make the personal and business lives of clients better, in their particular circumstances.

This all gives clear pointers as to what are, from the perspective of a law firm, the traits of The Perfect Lawyer. The Perfect Lawyer is not going far enough if they are proud merely of what they do for clients – they need to have a *dual pride* where there is also a pride in what they are doing for their business.

I refer to lawyers doing maximum work (as a team), catching all the time spent whilst that work is being done, billing all the time that has been caught, and getting all bills paid quickly. The firm needs its lawyers to maximise the profit *and cash* that their expertise, their time, and their files generate.

That gets the business ready for "wider" growth, where it rolls out a now-perfected business and cash-generation model. Until this point, a firm would be rolling out a flawed business model, and that "rolling out" could cost it dearly.

CHAPTER 10

ACHIEVING WIDER GROWTH?

Having secured "first growth" out of existing "assets" by now making maximum profit and cash on every existing and new case that the firm takes on, and by making that money without delays, and by securing maximum cases from every existing and every new client over time, the firm is well-armed to look at continued and wider growth.

Let's now look at how firms chase wider growth – and what they need from their lawyers to help them succeed here.

I have seen law firms try to "grow" their businesses in the following ways:

- Bringing in a new Partner (with a "following")
- Bringing in a team of lawyers from another firm
- Encouraging people to do more "BD"
- Opening a new practise area
- Opening a new office
- Increasing prices
- Merging with a local competitor
- Acquiring small local firms

- Pushing each team to have its own marketing plan
- Building a new website
- Designing new brochures
- Advertising or sponsorship campaigns
- Spend more on their marketing team
- Social media campaigns
- Press releases

Let's look at the strengths and weaknesses of some of these common "growth" strategies, particularly if they are not carefully managed. For even if they succeed, on their own, they don't necessarily bring the growth in the defined profit and cash terms that the Perfect Legal Business needs.

I do this so we can come to see what a law firm needs from its lawyers to ensure the right, wider growth is actually attained each and every year.

Bringing in new lawyers from other firms

Lateral hires (bringing in Partners or teams from other firms) can work. They don't always work, but I have seen some great examples of firms using a determined, focused recruitment programme as a main growth strategy. Some firms have this as the backbone of their growth aspirations.

There are some clear features present in such firms, though, which lead to these programmes being effective and successful, while other firms fail at it.

A commitment to a culture and a set of values and behaviours is key. That is carried through the recruitment programme by consistency in terms of assessment and in terms of the interviewer(s) – here, lawyers of random make-up are not being recruited in different parts of the firm by inconsistent interview panels that are also randomly made-up.

Once hired, new recruits are then well and truly inducted into the new firm. Induction here is about more than fire exits.

And wrong moves or behaviours on the part of the new arrivals are acted upon so that education and induction are an ongoing process, not a series of meetings that are signed off by the Head of HR or the office manager after a week.

Firms that make the growth-by-recruitment strategy work also have the ability to recognise when a new hire simply isn't working and maybe won't ever work, and such firms are ready, willing, and able to make a hard business decision to draw a line and terminate a new or recent hire.

And, finally, firms that successfully employ recruitment as a growth strategy recognise the cash implications of achieving growth in this way. Cash starts going out as soon as a lawyer starts work at a new firm – it is imperative that cash starts coming in quickly, too. So, a further benefit of strong cash behaviours at a law firm is that a sustained recruitment programme is possible.

If a firm doesn't have a set of values and behaviours that make up a clear culture, and/or does not recognise the potential cash impact of new hires, then "recruitment" as a growth strategy is very dangerous. It can lead to a short-term cash challenge and long-term cultural erosion.

Let's look at the cash dangers that a "growth-by-recruitment" strategy can bring if the hiring firm doesn't embrace the right cash behaviours and imbue them into every incoming lawyer from the outset.

It may be that at their former firms, the new lawyers, Partners, or team in question were rewarded, as is largely the way in our profession, for their *billing* levels. That's all you asked them about in the interview, right? (You mean you didn't ask them about debtor days, team Gross Margin, unbilled disbursements, utilisation rates, realisation rates, and WIP write-offs?)

So, the new lawyers start at your firm, and their salaries – which are, of course, paid in *cash* – start going out in the first month. If things go well, they start *billing* after a month or two or three, depending on the type of work they do. In some work-types, the delay before their billing starts can be much, much longer.

As we have seen, sending bills out causes a problem for their new firm. How quickly are their loyal clients used to *paying* those bills when the bills do eventually start getting sent out? What were the cash behaviours and disciplines of the lawyer at their previous firm? Do their clients (who may have cashflow challenges of their own) see this as an opportunity to have their suppliers (that's the new law firm) fund their business for longer?

Absent their bills being paid quickly, a few months of new salaries going out and that new lateral hire or that new team starting can cause their new firm real cash problems – even though their billing and thus their "profit" may look healthy.

The position is all the more damaging if the lawyers in question do what I call "long-tail" work – long commercial or property deals, or corporate deals or personal litigation work that is of a contingent nature, for example.

It doesn't take many of these new salaries before a firm's limited cash reserves get depleted in the face of locked-up WIP and/or unpaid bills – and all the while the firm is paying VAT on unpaid bills and tax on "unpaid bill" profit and "WIP uplift" profit. And let's not forget that recruitment agents' fees of typically 15-20% of the new lawyers' salaries will also have had to have been paid. That's a huge cash hit in itself.

As I say, though, some firms use the recruitment process really well as a vehicle for significant growth, but it is not always gold-plated and is not guaranteed to be successful.

Many firms will have been bowled over by the promised "followings" or the Business Development brilliance of lawyers and Partners they have interviewed, only for reality to fall a long way short of the rainbows they were promised.

Even when a new hire does deliver, a new Partner or team that is under pressure to perform (in the first instance, to open files) is not necessarily going to be committed to charging their long-standing clients "top dollar" for their work. They'll just be relieved to get another job in from a client who has followed them. The new lawyers are unlikely to be able to get their clients to follow them with assurances that hourly rates are going up and credit periods are going down.

On the contrary, the new lawyers may be hoping to coax their clients across to the new firm by telling them prices will be going down, and credit periods are going up.

I have seen very many examples of new Partners whose performance was celebrated – until Management looked at their "Debtors".

Securing wider growth by new and increased "Marketing" and "Business Development"

Law firms look favourably at lawyers who are good at Business Development and "Marketing". Inclinations and abilities, here, can be a facet of The Perfect Lawyer, from a firm's perspective.

However, let's look under this bonnet, too, as I do not believe that most firms are fully arming their lawyers to enable them to carry out really *effective* BD on behalf of the firm. It could be done better if the firm put a few building blocks in place first. Again, teamwork.

That would allow and enable *every* lawyer to do *effective* BD, not just those who are confident enough to walk into a room and not leave until they've got a business card from everyone in it.

In simplistic terms, one "star" BD lawyer can get, say, ten business cards on a busy night. *All* your lawyers doing proper BD on an ongoing basis (including those that would never see themselves as BD high-performers) can harvest many hundreds, and can leave a powerful message with each interaction.

And it's not the collecting of business cards that brings in the work – it's what happens after that.

On all these fronts, lawyers can indeed be perfect, but not without the support, courage, and direction of the firm.

I've always liked the saying, "Only half of all BD and Marketing works – but you sadly never know which half".

I believe that, when it comes to law firms, *more* than half of all BD and Marketing does *not* work. I believe a great deal more than half doesn't work and is a waste of time, money, energy, and of the goodwill that a firm's people invest in it.

If we step outside the legal sector for a moment, I'll show you what I mean.

Imagine two companies that both make cars, where there is nothing different between the cars of Company A and the cars of Company B. They are priced roughly the same, too. As it happens, the cars of both Company A and Company B break down from time to time.

Sometimes, you get a good one, sometimes you get a bad one.

Let's imagine how the meeting between the Senior Management team at Company A, their Marketing team, and their Sales team, goes.

It would be usual for the CEO to demand more and more Marketing and more and more Sales effort, to get sales up. The more marketing, the better, right? But imagine you're in the Marketing or Sales team there. You'd be faced with a huge challenge: "What on earth can we say about our cars that'll get people to buy them?"

They're in a fix, as they can't differentiate their cars in any way from those of Company B. How amazing it would be if they could boast about the quality and reliability of their cars – what a differentiator that would be. But Company A's cars break down too.

So, what's left in terms of ammunition that they can use? Not much, really. Maybe "Our cars are cheaper"?

Or maybe they could try what lots of law firms try – they could tell customers how long they've been in business. Or they could showcase the industry awards they've won. Or they could boast about being a really *big* car maker – in the Top 200 carmakers in the country, perhaps.

But absent any real differentiators between their cars and those of their competitors – differentiators that really benefit customers – you can see that the Marketing people have an uphill struggle.

That's precisely how it is for the Marketing people in many law firms.

And that is precisely how it is for lawyers in a law firm, too. They are expected to "do BD" but haven't got any "knockout" differentiators to boast of.

In very general terms, I think we can divide "Marketing" (in the sense that it is used in law firms) into Part 1 and Part 2.

- Part 1 is the design and the engineering of real differentiators – outstanding aspects that set a firm apart in a crowded marketplace, which are of real value to clients.

- Part 2 is the broadcasting of the firm's messages to existing and potential clients.

I have rarely seen *any* Part 1 work *at all* taking place at a law firm. Instead, without building any real brand or promise or differentiators, law firms spend a fortune on Part 2 activities. In reality, a fortune is spent shouting about, well, not much at all.

In the business world more widely, the Marketing people often lead the way. They have input into the *what* and also into the *how* and into the *why* of a business. They help to shape the culture, the values, the design, and the pricing of goods and services.

They thus engineer a brand and help to build differentiators that give a boost to the business's marketing and Business Development efforts. And they help to train the whole team to convey the message "out there".

In the example given above, it would not be unusual for the Marketing people at Company A to engage with the CEO to underline for him or her that the real brand opportunity in the scenario I have outlined was to build a car that *didn't* break down.

Imagine the messaging that could then be broadcast. "Our cars will always get you there!" That would be their equivalent of the Service Pledge that we looked at in Chapter 1.

And guess what could happen to the price of their cars and the number that they sold.

In law firms, typically because of the respective seniority of Partners and Marketing people that still exists in most firms, the Marketing people are led by the lawyers and do what the lawyers ask them – "Let's have a seminar", "I want a cheese & wine evening", or "Let's write an article", etc.

And then nothing arrives from the lawyers until the last minute. And no one's ever sure who to invite to events once they've been organised.

It can be pretty ad hoc, but it doesn't cause any real problems because that's exactly what's going on at competitor firms. A law firm's main advantage is that all of its competitors are law firms.

The Marketing team usually just doesn't have the standing to say, for example, "Stop! Why don't we completely redesign the service that we offer clients, so that we innovate to deliver a truly great service – every lawyer, every time. So that our car gets there every time. That'll make us a brand with a promise that will have people flocking to us, and that will be *the* differentiator in the legal market. We can charge a fortune for it".

Absent that kind of standing on the part of the Marketing team in a law firm, what *can* the Marketing people possibly say that sets *their* lawyers apart from those of other law firms?

And what *can* the lawyers themselves, who are charged with doing "Business Development" and "Networking", say that is going to first capture someone's interest at a networking event and then enable that contact to be nurtured so that they become a life-long client, apart from "We're really good" or "We're really cheap"?

When we look at law firm differentiators, below, you can see exactly what law firms currently say to stand out in a crowded marketplace.

Pursuing wider growth by driving each team to undertake marketing and BD efforts

It is not uncommon for each team in a law firm to be allocated its own Marketing budget. The teams are expected to use that money – and a considerable amount of their lawyers' time (in office hours and out of office hours) – to undertake "BD" activities to generate work *for their team.*

The outputs of that process can be curious. The firm's Employment team, for example, could be targeting a company on a local business park, and would be writing to them, inviting them to events, sending them briefings and the like. And the Dispute Resolution team could be writing to them as well. And the Real Estate team. And the Corporate team. And the Debt Recovery team.

Each team is promoting itself. And, of course, the aim of each is to win "a new case for their team" rather than "a new *client* for the firm". The aim is mainly to win what I call Matter 1, or ".001", for a new client. Trumpets sound when that happens.

But it's hard work to win a new client without any powerful differentiators. Any conversations with prospective clients can gravitate towards price – and that's *if* – a big *if* – the client has a need for those services at that time.

And whilst this is going on, there are lots of clients of the Employment team that the Real Estate team would love to act for. And lots of clients of the Dispute Resolution team that the Employment team would love to act for. And on it goes.

I do not believe that team-by-team marketing is the best way to grow a legal business in a sustainable way – a team might do well now and again, but huge firm-wide opportunities are missed.

It is when the firm and the various teams all work together that magic can happen. Islands doing their own thing (be they teams or individual lawyers) can only ever have limited results in comparison.

New brochures

Has your firm got cupboards full of brochures that teams or individual lawyers wanted, but which have not been used? Many a firm has. There are two main things I would say about brochures.

1. What's in them that sets your firm apart from other firms?

2. What is going to be done with the brochures?

The main plan for brochures is usually to hand them out to prospective new clients. But do you actually really need new clients?

I worked with a law firm that was very proud of its new, very expensive brochure. They had spent a lot of money and time on it. I asked the Partners to put their hands up if they had ten or more files on their desk that they simply couldn't get around to working on. They all put their hand up. Is it me?

And if you do hand them out, will it achieve anything? What's in them? I tell the story in this book about the superb corporate client who asked me (whilst he was beauty-parading my firm against two esteemed competitor law firms) why he, his family, and his company should use my firm. I said five words, and he said, "I'm all yours". My five words were "Have a look at that", as I passed him a list of our differentiators. They were on a piece of A4 paper.

Achieving wider growth by opening up a new practise area

This is often tried, but it comes with risks. Many an exciting new venture has failed.

The main risks are the cash impact, the risks to your reputation, and the risks to your Professional Indemnity Insurance policy.

Is there any certainty that the new lawyer will start bringing cash in quickly (i.e., don't just look at when they'll start sending bills out), and will that cash be more than you are paying them?

As it's a new area of law for your firm, who's going to monitor the quality and risk profile of their clients and the lawyer's work?

If a firm sets out on a mission to transform itself from a firm offering a narrow range of legal services to one offering "the full range of legal services", these issues are repeated – over and over again. "Sticking to your knitting", and staying with what you are best at, is an extremely compelling and low-risk business strategy – and your chances of enjoying the real differentiator of being "the best" are higher than they might be if you are made up of a series of bolt-on lawyers from disparate legal backgrounds.

Opening a new office

I did this, and I like it as a growth strategy. When it comes to opening a new office in a new town, the obvious options are:

- to go into that new location "cold", with your own new office and your own people – one of your existing lawyers who lives there, perhaps, or

- bring in a "star" lawyer from a local firm who'll open doors for you in that new location, or

- acquire or merge with an established firm in that location

Going back to the example I gave of the two companies that make cars, you might have Company A and Company B both making cars in a town, with no differentiators to boost either and nothing really between them. But now, Company C has joined the fray (i.e., a new law firm comes into the local marketplace). If Company C doesn't have any differentiators either, how on earth is it going to break into the market presently served by Company A and Company B? Doesn't the arrival of Company C just increase the downward pressure on prices for all three businesses?

If Company C *does* have real differentiators, though, then the local status quo gets blown apart. Imagine if, as a law firm, you did have real differentiators that would make clients choose you, whatever your prices, as well as making local lawyers choose you as their employer. You'd be able to go into all those towns and cities and trump the status quo that clients and lawyers there had become used to.

It would be like Company C arriving in a new town, shouting, "Our cars never break down". This is where the Service Pledge comes in.

My work with law firms who have growth aspirations often starts with their desire to "have more locations" but it quickly morphs into us working together to get them "battle ready" first, including by strengthening existing, and engineering new, differentiators, and by making sure that they make maximum profit and cash – and soon – on every case that they take on. They can *then* roll out a much stronger business model into new territories.

I urge them to hold off from entering new markets until they look more like The Perfect Legal Business (in all the ways this book explores) and only then to "press the button". When they do subsequently press the button, the risks are profoundly lower and the prospects of success are significantly higher.

Achieving growth by merging with local competitors

I am not talking here about the various large, well-funded (often, listed) businesses that are currently undertaking a programme of acquisitions of other law firms. I am mainly referring here, for example, to two (or more) firms in a town or city that decide to throw their lot in together after decades of competing against each other.

I once received a call from the Managing Partner of a competitor firm. Verbatim, the call went like this:

Him: "It's time you brought your firm into mine, Simon."

Me: "Why?"

Him: "Well, if you do, we'll have a turnover of £50 million."

Me: "I asked why?"

Him: "Simon – you're not listening!"

Being big is not a sound and effective strategy. And if you add one firm with no differentiators to another firm with no differentiators, and add cultural and behavioural differences and a host of fudges to make sure no one felt left out of ownership or management, you won't always create a secure and sustainable "growth" beast.

Adding one flawed business to another doesn't fix either. And examples abound of mergers where, decades later, you can still see the two distinct groups of people.

These things can work, but sometimes they don't. And then it's too late.

Achieving growth by increasing prices

A lack of what I call "Pride in Pricing" is very evident as I travel around law firms. It is one of the many mistakes I made as a Managing Partner.

Lawyers of all levels across my firm were responsible for their own pricing, and we had no collective confidence in pricing our services at a level commensurate with what we were offering. We truly had a great team delivering a great service – every lawyer, every time – but I don't think we charged enough for that in hindsight. We really were giving a Bentley service for a Volkswagen price.

Knowing what I know now, I believe it perfectly fair to charge a high price for a great service. If a client doesn't want to pay that price, they are free to choose another firm. The better the service (in terms of both legal expertise and in delivery of that expertise), the higher the price should be.

What some firms do, though, is just try to raise their prices without raising their game. Raising prices gets you more money per case, for a while, but I have seen it leave unaddressed various deep-rooted problems, such as:

- Staff might still be leaving

- The firm might be unable to attract new talent

- The firm still has no differentiators

- Client service levels could still be poor

- Cross-selling and cross-caring to clients is absent

Higher prices are not, in themselves, a formula for sustained success.

I worked for a while with a firm whose boast was that they were the dearest firm in their city. They couldn't explain to clients why they were dearest – they couldn't justify their high prices with any compelling differentiators. In fact, in some places, their service levels were downright awful. Their business was struggling. Raising prices is not a "quick fix" panacea.

Summary of the "usual" growth options

Accepting that The Perfect Legal Business needs wider growth that will bring growth in both profit and cash, we have cantered around the various common trails that law firms blaze in pursuit of that growth.

I hope I have been able to demonstrate that many of the most popular freeways to growth are pitted with potholes. They come with cost, risk, and uncertainty.

The Perfect Legal Business and its lawyers do none of these things, yet.

It recognises that there are cheaper, safer, and more effective, local, sustainable, attainable, profitable, and cash-rich ways of securing the necessary wider growth. These require that the law firm and the lawyers work together in partnership.

CHAPTER 11

GROWING THE BUSINESS IN THE RIGHT WAY

The Perfect Legal Business and its lawyers start and continue by looking inwards.

The firm looks at itself to get in place and keep in place the foundations that will serve it and its people – and its existing and a growing number of new clients – very well when it does start looking outwards (including in the ways I listed above) in due course.

It starts and then relentlessly works with its lawyers to perfect the fundamentals of a legal business. It is these that are the foundations for real growth. They never go away.

All too often, in rolling its business model out, a law firm is rolling out a flawed model, and the very "success" of that rolling-out will bring the law firm [cash] pain, rather than pleasure.

I was guilty of this – under my drive and direction, my firm rolled out a business model that was hugely successful on some levels. It had powerful differentiators, no shortage of clients and work, and no shortage of "top drawer" talent in our legal and Business Support teams. We delivered a great service –

every lawyer, every time – and we got more and more work from our many existing and new clients.

But that's not enough if you are to be The Perfect Legal Business. We were indeed "the perfect firm of solicitors, from a client's perspective", but the more we rolled out our "successful" model, the higher the pressure on our business, because we didn't have our profit, and more importantly, our cash behaviours, right.

Whether a business achieves all the necessary things *is in the hands of its lawyers*.

If a firm's lawyers don't embrace and do the fundamental things, they will adversely affect the boat's direction and speed.

Let's now take the things we did right in my firm, and the things we did wrong but which I have seen done right at successful firms and which I have since helped other firms to do right.

In doing this, we can bring together the pieces of the jigsaw that will enable The Perfect Legal Business to successfully pursue sustained and wider growth, and this will define what The Perfect Lawyers in that business look like and how they need to act.

1. BUILD DIFFERENTIATORS

Before the Perfect Legal Business shouts about itself in the many forms and across the many forums that exist nowadays, it builds qualitative *differentiators* that make it stand out to clients in what is a crowded marketplace.

One of the two best business stories I have ever heard rammed home the importance of differentiators to me.

Credit for the story goes to a BBC "Business Programme" presenter who told the story to a business audience at an event I was at in Reading a few years ago.

He was strolling one evening along the Keys in Florida. He saw a series of rickety, wooden stalls from which various people were selling freshly-caught lobsters. All the stalls still had lobsters on them and the stallholders were chatting amongst themselves. All the stalls, that is, except one... he was packing up to go home. The speaker was intrigued, and he approached the stallholder.

"You're all sold out?"

"Yup."

"Same lobsters as the others?"

"Yup."

"From the same boat?"

"Yup."

"And the same price as the other stalls?"

"Yup."

"So why are you sold out and they're not?"

"Check this out", at which point the stallholder lifted the blackboard that had been on his stall all day. It read:

HAVE YOU TRIED LOBSTER IN LEMON?

BAKE THE LOBSTER FOR 2 HOURS, WITH 4 SLICED LEMONS.

FREE LEMONS WITH ALL MY LOBSTERS.

The BBC speaker then turned to the business audience and calmly asked, "Let me ask all of you – where are *your* lemons?"

No lemons – no standing out from the crowd. The lemons cost the stallholder five cents each, but they were a knockout differentiator in that particular marketplace.

The Perfect Legal Business embraces this approach. With its lawyers and indeed all its people, it designs and engineers substantive, meaningful differentiators. And saying you have differentiators is one thing – delivering on them constantly is another. Having designed and engineered differentiators, the Perfect Legal Business commits itself to delivering on them consistently, and its lawyers dedicate themselves to *personally* and *collectively* doing so.

This is where The Perfect Lawyers come in – they invest time and passion in helping the firm design its differentiators and commit to delivering on them, not reverting to how they've always done things as soon as no one is looking. With all its lawyers delivering on its brand, the firm can make a loud promise to the external world.

All lawyers doing things the same, good way – all the time – is the essence of a *brand*. A brand is a promise. People buy brands and people stay with brands. People don't question the price of brands.

But what should the differentiators be that the lawyers help to build and then deliver on? Let's look at the "differentiators" that law firms typically use – at what law firms *say* their lemons are to help them stand out in a crowded marketplace.

Common law firm "differentiators" (as seen on real law firm websites)

- We're unlike any other law firm [I couldn't see why]

- We're a law firm like no other [Again, I couldn't see why]

- We offer an excellent service [Really? So you have no files sitting on desks for weeks, waiting?]

- Award-winning [So what? Will your lawyers push my case and return my calls?]

- Honest [I should think so!]

- Expert [I should hope so!]

- Lawyers you can trust [Again – I should hope so]

- Friendly [I've got enough friends – I want a good *lawyer*]

- We try to secure the best result for you [I should think so!]

- We work actively for you [I would hope so!]

- We opened in 1846 [Great – but do you push and tell now?]

- Tailored legal services [Really? I bet you still do it all your way!]

- We're a Top 100 firm [So, only 99 other firms like you?]

- We're a Legal 500 firm [So, only 499 other firms like you!?]

Are any of the above differentiators? No, not really. It is genuinely very, very hard to find anything at all, when looking at law firm websites, that is truly a differentiator.

I demonstrate the power of differentiators in this book with the story above of how I won the work of a lovely client, with only five words. He never even asked about prices.

Whilst I was Managing Partner, I had lunch with the Managing Partner of a competitor (and far more glamorous and illustrious) law firm. I asked that Managing Partner why a client should use their firm. The Managing Partner looked at me for a long time, puzzled, in total silence.

My comment to them was, "Crikey – if *you* can't tell me why a client should use your firm, how can your people be expected to be out there marketing and developing business for you?"

Their reply was, "Go on then – why should anyone use *your* firm?" I replied immediately, "Because we offer every area of law, we deliver a great service – every lawyer, every time, guaranteed – and we look after our clients proactively".

Knockout. And every one of our 200 or so people would have given – and believed in – the same answer.

I believe that "service" is the differentiator *par excellence*, and I have looked in this book at how a law firm and its lawyers can and should arrive at a Service Pledge that they move heaven and earth to constantly deliver on.

That is a compelling differentiator that trumps anything on the list above.

2. MAKE MAXIMUM PROFIT *AND CASH, AND SOON,* FOR DELIVERING THAT AMAZING SERVICE

From the outset, and throughout all its efforts and initiatives, this is a pillar of The Perfect Legal Business.

Yes, I mean making maximum profit on each case. But I mean more than that. I also mean making that profit *soon.* There is a time element here. It's no good if the law firm will make good money on a case some day. It needs to make that good money *this financial year,* otherwise it doesn't count towards a firm's success, where success is measured in "profit per financial year".

When it comes to profit and cash, McDonalds – for example – has got it easy. Not so for us. The "profit and cash journey" for law firms is not short, simple, or straight. It is made up of six separate steps, or challenges. The firm and its lawyers have to get all of them right. The chain breaks down at any of its links.

Of course, it's not the firm that is "on the ground" at each of these links. It is the individual lawyers who are there. They can deliver perfectly on this at each stage, or they can do things in an imperfect, flawed way. The six steps are as follows:

Step 1 – Price the work at the right level

My firm had every reason to have "Pride in Pricing" – more reason than any firm I know – but we didn't translate the power of our brand and our differentiators into price differentials between us and other firms (in terms of either our fixed prices or our hourly rates). It never occurred to me that we might be able to adopt and instil a confidence across the firm that what we were offering was special and that clients should therefore pay a "Bentley" price for it.

The Perfect Lawyer, having first helped the firm to design its differentiators (i.e., the firm's Service Pledge), and who is now helping the firm to deliver on it, has "Pride in Pricing" and does not sell the expertise of the firm cheaply. This is one of the golden "client" rules I referred to earlier.

Step 2 – Define retainers and charge extra fees for extra work

Step 2 is another of the golden "client" rules mentioned earlier.

We did this, but it was more to reduce the risk of Professional Indemnity claims against us, rather than to make sure that we were paid for any extra work a file needed, and to make sure that we never did *any* work for free.

I have seen firms use this tool to great effect, where vertical and horizontal definitions are put in place in the retainer to make sure the firm always gets paid for *all* the work it does. By vertical lines, I mean that if the extent of the job widens, extra charges will kick in. By horizontal lines, I mean that regardless of whether the job changes, if it goes beyond a certain date, extra charges will kick in, or if time costs exceed the fixed price by a certain percentage, extra costs kick in.

Again, it is usually down to the individual lawyer scoping a job properly and designing a retainer that makes clear what work and time is covered and what work and time is not covered. It's also, of course, then down to the individual lawyer to police files they are working on and to catch any mission-creep as soon as it arises.

Step 3 – Actually doing the work, and properly

Lawyers work hard. They will take a new file on, committed to working on it. However, they were usually too busy even before that new file came in, so now other files move to the back of the desk, and are not worked on, or need to have time on them snatched. This is not the lawyer's problem; it is the team's and the firm's problem.

There's no money to be made from storage. If a file isn't being worked on, it's costing you money, not earning you money. It's also costing you your good name. Daylight (on a file) is the best generator of fees.

But there's "working on a file" and there's "working on a file". Snatching a few minutes on a file because the client has chased you or because a deadline is approaching is a far cry from measured, thoughtful, detailed work on a file.

A firm often needs more lawyers (or a better team structure) than it needs more files.

It is for the firm, usually through an active Team Leader, to assess whether all the vessels in a team are full, and if they are, new vessels need to be brought in. Only then can all the new work be done and done properly.

I said above that it's not just about making maximum profit on a case. That profit has to be made *soon*. Pay rises and bonuses can't be paid out of full pipelines – they are paid out of billed files. To make maximum money, and soon, the Team Leaders and the firm as a whole need to constantly create and top-up lawyer capacity to ensure that all cases are worked on properly all the time.

Step 4 – Record all the time you spend on a file (Utilisation)

This one is very much down to the individual lawyer.

Charging the client by applying an hourly rate to the time recorded has not gone away, far from it. From what I see at the many law firms that I work with, depending on work-types, this is still the mainstay of legal business.

Simply put, the more chargeable hours a law firm's lawyers *do and record* (for they are different things), the better the opportunity to generate maximum profit and cash "down the line".

I believe that lawyers *do* far more hours than they *record*. I often see a frustration on the part of Management but also on the part of lawyers themselves, where lawyers record no more than say 3 or 4 chargeable hours in a day that saw them start work at 8 am, work through their lunch, toil hard all day, and go home in the evening.

One reason for this is that lawyers may simply have too many files. It's hard to catch all the time you spend on a range of files when you are dashing from file to file to file.

It might also be because, in fact, the real-world priority in a firm is not to "record as many chargeable hours as possible". Every lawyer may well have a "chargeable hours" target – commonly 5 a day, or 1,200 a year – but all the reporting and monitoring and applauding and rewarding (and barking) that goes on might be around something completely different. Usually, it's "billing".

As I did at my firm, many firms focus on the lawyers' *output* target of "bills raised" instead of focusing on the lawyers' first *input* target, namely "the number of chargeable hours *done and recorded*".

The result of this is that billing can be much less than it might otherwise be, and hitting billing targets, rather than a desire to hit *efficient, maximum production*, is what drives lawyers, teams, and Team Leaders.

You can usually hit normal billing targets without getting anywhere near target chargeable hours. Inefficiency, indeed failure, is built into the financial system. It shouldn't be.

In the most general of terms, you might have a three-year qualified solicitor who is paid, say, £40,000 a year. Their hourly rate might be £180 an hour. If they were to focus on recording time in a drive to hit a "chargeable hours" target, then they could easily bill over £200,000 a year without working past 5 pm.

But often what drives them and the team and the firm is a different target – a *billing* target, and there is a broad view in the legal profession that billings (B) and salaries (S) are the two sides of an equation where $B = 3 \times S$.

This imposes an artificial cap on the billings that lawyers can contemplate and that firms require of their lawyers. In this example, the lawyer might feel it reasonable if they are asked to bill around £120,000, but less reasonable if they are asked to bill over £200,000, in light of the salary they are on. But, working efficiently, they can bill £120,000 by stopping work at lunchtime.

If, instead of focusing on the *output* of billings, a firm focuses on (and reports on and rewards) the *input* of chargeable hours, the result could – in due course – be much higher billings from the same lawyers with the same cases. That means higher profits that can and should feed into the healthy pay rises that the lawyers want.

As you will see below, this is the guaranteed way to get a team's Gross Profit Margin to increase.

Setting targets (and rewards) on the input side (time recording) rather than on the output side (billing) would encourage lawyers to be more efficient in catching all the time they undoubtedly already spend on files. The upside is much improved financial performance by them individually, by their team, and by their firm as a whole. They would be entitled to expect that as the tide came in, all the boats would rise, and they would benefit financially.

At my firm, yes, we had a "chargeable hours" target and yes, the chargeable hours (or Utilisation) data appeared somewhere on a crowded spreadsheet every month, but frankly, all I was interested in was whether each team had hit their (low) billing (output) target each month.

By focusing on the "time recording" input instead of the "billing" output, you can easily move towards a situation where B = 4 x S or even B = 5 x S, so that the extra revenue drops straight to the bottom line. And you can achieve this without the lawyers doing any more work than they are already doing. The result is a strong business that offers more security, more reward, and more opportunities to its people.

As the import of this becomes clear, you will see that this is actually a serious problem for a law firm. It pays a lawyer to do, to record, and to bill around 5 chargeable hours a day. If a lawyer only does 4 a day, or does many hours a day but only records 4 of them (which data shows would actually be above the national average for recorded hours in the UK), they are giving the business only 80% Utilisation. That's a huge cost to the business.

The real problem, though, is that there's further bad news coming along the tracks when we look at what happens next.

Step 5 – Bill all the time that is recorded (Realisation, or Recovery)

It's no use doing and recording lots of hours on a file (so that your Utilisation figures are good) that you then write off when it comes to doing a bill. The aim at The Perfect Legal Business is also to bill all the time that is recorded on a file. That is, to have a 100% *Realisation* rate.

There might be a number of reasons why, say, there's £1,000 on the billing guide but a bill is raised for only £750. These could include an element of double-charging if the file has been transferred between lawyers with consequent reading-in, or mistakes were made that obviously can't be charged for. But they can also include sympathy for the client or lack of "Pride in Pricing" on the part of the lawyer when the price or costs estimate was given at the outset.

I recall being guilty of discounting when I did the cross-team billing every month for a household-name client for whom we were carrying out a lot of work across various teams at any one time. I recall looking for opportunities to offer discounts and reductions.

I always wanted to "throw a bit in" in return for all the other work that we were charging for. I had no reason whatsoever to do that – we were blowing the client away with an amazing cross-firm service that they'd never seen before. I have seen many firms – where I look at the reasons behind low Realisation rates – who do the same.

In the same way that low Utilisation "input" rates are overlooked if the "output" *billing* levels are in line with a billing target (which in turn is based only on the B = 3 x S equation), so too are low Realisation rates overlooked. I was guilty of this when I was Managing Partner. Nothing mattered, provided the (low) output billing targets were hit.

But now consider this: if a lawyer's time recording (Utilisation) is only at say 80%, and the lawyer then only realises or recovers 75% of the time that is recorded on files when it comes to billing, then their overall billing and profit efficiency is 75% of 80%, so only **60%!**

In short, it's as if they're going home at lunchtime. They're obviously not, but the financial result here is not enabling the lawyer to truly benefit in cash and progression terms from their hard work. There needs to be a pride here, too, on the part of the lawyer – "No one gets my expertise and my hard work for free – ever! And I'm certainly not going to work for free for about half my time!"

The deal between law firm and lawyer should be a clear one, where a lawyer stepping out from under the "B = 3 x S" umbrella will see clear reward and progression.

"Ah yes", I hear some lawyers say, "none of this applies to me as all of my work is fixed-fee work". They couldn't be more wrong.

If lawyers price a fixed-fee job at say £1,000, and it always takes £1,500 of time (so that Utilisation rates are high as the lawyers work hard to deal with the cases but the Realisation rates are low because the price does not take into account all the time the job needs) then the challenge in that fixed-fee work is to use your differentiators and the Utilisation and Realisation data to get the low fixed price up.

It is, at the very least, worth trying to engage with the client to show them the problem and, over time, to try to reduce the problem by moving the fixed fee first to, say, £1,100, then to £1,250, and then to £1,500, or more directly.

The Realisation rate here will go up at each stage. The way to get the price up is to have an explanation for the client as to why the price needs to be higher – by pointing to the data and to your differentiators, the greatest of which will be your expertise, your familiarity with their work, and your Service Pledge. Do the clients really want to go back out into the marketplace and have to educate a new firm about their cases or their business, and run the risk of engaging a firm that neither pushes nor tells?

What should Utilisation rates and Realisation rates be? The answer is always simply "Higher!" That's the genuine answer – higher. If Team Leaders work with their individual lawyers, within a framework where these inputs are "front of house" and are monitored, tracked, and rewarded as highly as the billing output was previously, they can slowly but surely get their Utilisation rates up and their Realisation rates up, and the result will be an increase in the output of billing and in the team's profitability – see Gross Profit, below. All without any additional work being done.

Step 6 – Getting paid quickly

This was the last of the golden "client" rules that we looked at above. There's no point having the confidence to quote high prices, and of having a culture where service levels are paramount, and where the inputs of Utilisation and Realisation are more important than the output of billing, only for that apparatus to result in more and more larger and larger bills finding a home (and travelling to the right) in the "Aged Debtors" list.

The more bills and the bigger the bills on this list, the more harm it will do to the business. Think of all the VAT and all the tax on "profit" that the firm is having to pay! Growth in billing levels, as I hope is clear from earlier chapters, can cause real pain if the bills aren't paid quickly.

In summary, when it comes to profit and cash, The Perfect Legal Business delivers an amazing service, but it demands in return a good price, in cash, from the clients. It ensures maximum profit by having Pride in Pricing at the outset, by making sure there are enough lawyers to do the work properly, and by focusing on the lawyers' inputs rather than their outputs as the cases progress. It then avoids undermining the whole show by the lawyers all having a deep-seated "Cash Commitment".

Now that I am a disciple that worships at the altar of fee-earner inputs rather than outputs, I help firms to buy into this new approach and to get all their lawyers to strive to become more effective and efficient at turning *all* their hard work and great service into profit and cash – and then to go home on time.

I have seen examples with firms I have worked with where, as quickly as Month #1 of the "new way", lawyer data can improve, so that team performances can go up, with the effect that the firm's profit goes up. Firms regularly have record years – without winning new clients or embarking on expensive marketing campaigns and without anyone working any harder or longer. Everyone just works smarter.

In one case that jumps to mind, we saw the firm's profitability go up every month for the next six months, including a December without a single new lawyer or any new marketing initiative or influx of new cases. Record years are routine.

The Perfect Legal Business is a high-profit, cash business, not a turnover-based credit business. It has the confidence to only take on work that is priced profitably, and to tell clients at the outset that they have to pay their bills on time or they can't enjoy the great service the law firm offers.

3. RUN THE BUSINESS AS A SERIES OF SEPARATE BUSINESSES – TEAMS AND TEAM LEADERS

I need to talk about Team Leaders. And I do mean "Team Leaders". I don't like the title "Head of Department" or "HoD". It suggests someone whose job is to preserve everything "just as it is".

A "Team Leader", on the other hand, should do what it says on the tin. They should build a team that exhibits *team* behaviours and which the Team Leader actively *leads* to higher and better ground. It is a far more dynamic state of affairs.

In the drive to increase the profitability and cash reserves of The Perfect Legal Business year after year, the firm's Management recognises that a law firm is usually not one business, but many.

Each area of law, and thus each team, has its own pressures and opportunities. The way to upgrade the profit and cash performance of the whole firm is to focus on each team individually.

However, Management simply cannot push all the required aspects that need to be pushed continually across all teams and across all the lawyers in each team.

Frankly, Management is unlikely to fully understand the intricacies of each team's commercial environment and marketplace in the way that a team's members might. And they are unlikely to command the same respect that someone from that "world" will.

A law firm that has the Managing Partner doing everything, or where the Managing Partner or CEO or the Finance Director has to liaise with all people at all levels across all teams and offices, to make sure all these aspects move forward all the time, will have limited prospects of sustained success. The firm's Management will become spread thinner and thinner. That kind of model is not scalable.

What is needed is effective *Middle* Management – otherwise known as Team Leaders. They are one of the real keys to the success of The Perfect Legal Business, particularly as it gets bigger.

Often, the contributions expected of a Team Leader in a law firm are not profit-, cash-, or growth-related. It's not always clear what the role and responsibility of a Team Leader is! What should each Team Leader be focusing on? I offer the following as a suggested agenda for focused, monthly team meetings that push all the right things:

Monthly Team Meetings Agenda	
Workloads	Do we have the right number and seniority of lawyers? Anyone got too much or not enough work? Senior lawyers doing junior tasks? Need more juniors/seniors?
All files being worked on as necessary – storage being avoided?	Are we snatching time on some files?

Monthly Team Meetings Agenda	
Support Staff	Are our lawyers dealing with non-chargeable admin? More profitable to get someone in to free lawyers up? Any bottlenecks, e.g., file-opening, typing?
Fee-earner inputs – Utilisation & Realisation	Are we recording good hours and billing them all?
Our team's gross margin	Heading in a good direction?
Existing debtors	Current state of printouts / target for next month's meeting
New debtor issues arising?	Are we making the same mistakes again?
Client engagement re: pricing / defining retainer / payment	Are we doing this? Feedback / share experiences
Service levels	Are we delivering on the firm's Service Pledge?
Have we referred any clients to other teams?	How was their response and service?
Have other teams referred clients to us?	How was our response and service?

On one side, the Team Leaders engage with their team in these ways to ensure that the team delivers on all the hard and soft aspects of The Perfect Legal Business. On the other side, the Team Leaders engage monthly *as a group* with the Senior Management Team to report on their team's progress and performance against the requirements that the centre of the business has of it.

A main Team Leader function is *active* production management. Let's go back to the example of the companies that make cars that I used earlier in the book. In their factories, the parts arrive at one end of the building and there is a carefully-crafted process – and timetable – that is designed to convert the parts into finished cars at the other end, as fast as possible. There are people whose role it is to time each part of the process, and to innovate and organise and marshal resources to get those times down and to make sure that quality stays "up". That way, having paid "money out", the business benefits from "money in" sooner rather than later. It is all, as it always is, about *cash, and soon.*

Now, compare that to what often happens in a law firm. Lots of cases come in at one end of a team, and then, all too often, production is not managed at all. Cases are left on (or under) a lawyer's desk, to be given attention when the lawyer can find the time or when something urgent arises on a file (or when a client rings to complain). Production management is left to each lawyer.

Lawyers are often simply too busy to do anything other than work at 100 mph and fight fires. Client service can never be consistent enough to constitute a "brand".

The firm can never benefit from the client loyalty and "Pride in Pricing" that would come from that, and the chances of wringing maximum money out of a file, let alone doing that soon, and let alone wringing a lifetime's value out of a client (and recruiting them into your sales team), are much reduced.

A Team Leader can take production management out of the hands of the individual lawyers and introduce meaningful production management by having the right team structure in place (by having what I call in this book good "lieutenant" lawyers that the senior lawyers trust, and by having sufficient "vessels"), by careful allocation of existing and new work, and by deft use of much-underused reports like the Inactivity Report or the Aged WIP report. These are all perfect production management tools.

Managed in this way, the various lawyers at differing levels can do great work on the team's files (instead of snatching "one unit" here and there), and the Team Leader can engage with them in what are effectively "production discussions" about the work needed on files, about the WIP on their Aged WIP reports, and to get all WIP billed as soon as possible.

This makes sure cases don't go into storage. And files carrying big blocks of WIP that can't be billed yet, because more work is first needed on the file, can be identified and given the required attention.

In light of the very varied nature of a Team Leader's role and responsibilities, taking into account all the hard and soft responsibilities of a Team Leader in The Perfect Legal Business, you may find it surprising to hear that the success or otherwise of a team of lawyers and their Team Leader, in business terms, can be measured by a single number.

The Team Leader, and the whole team, can have a simple speedometer on which they can see how they are doing. It is the $E = MC^2$ of the legal world.

4. GET TEAMS TO FOCUS ON THE ULTIMATE SPEEDOMETER

There's a very useful "speedometer" that you can use that tells you exactly how efficient a team of lawyers is at making profit, and whether their efforts to increase that profit are working. It's called the team's Gross Profit Margin, or "Gross Margin" for short.

I had the real pleasure of spending some time with a national "Head" of a highly successful global law firm a while back. This person was like a Team Leader, but on a massive scale. As part of the global firm's "middle management", every month he had to report to HQ (which was in another country) by email, on the financial performance of his part of this massive business.

His financial report each month was in a standard form. *It consisted of a single number.*

If I asked you, "Which business makes the most profit – BP, or your local corner shop?", you'd think that it was a ridiculous question, and indeed it is. There is no useful comparison that can be made between the profits in £ Sterling made by BP, and those made by the corner shop.

However, if I put the question another way, it becomes much more meaningful. "Between BP and your local corner shop, which is the most profitable?"

There is a universally-recognised number that is used the world over to measure the profit-making *efficiency* of a business or part of a business. It is called Gross Margin. It is a single number, expressed as *a percentage*.

It allows you to compare the profit-making efficiency of a global business to that of a small local business. Businesses the world over are obsessed with it. It drives all that they do.

It does not feature heavily, if at all, at most law firms. For us as a profession, *billing* is everything. Turnover! That completely obscures any understanding of a team or a firm's real profit, as we have seen. It's also not a good instrument to stimulate change and business improvement.

Team Gross Margins often appear on the printouts that a Finance team prepares and publishes every month, but they're frequently hidden amongst thousands of other numbers about billing, rather than being the compass and the engine room of each team.

So, what is Gross Margin, what is needed to get it to improve, and what is the lawyers' contribution here?

If you want to work out how much *profit* a team makes in £ Sterling, you simply deduct their salaries (including a sensible notional salary for any non-employee Equity Partner in the team) from their billings. That gives you what's called their *Gross* Profit – and it is measured in £ Sterling.

That's not the *overall* profit that the firm makes out of that team, as it doesn't yet take account of central costs and overheads that the business incurs for them, like rent, rates, gas, electricity, and so on. We exclude those things for this exercise as whilst the team can control their billings and salaries, it can't control what is spent decorating the reception areas, etc.

But when looking for a speedometer that can really help us to change things, we aren't interested in this Gross *Profit* measured in £ Sterling. We aren't looking here at actual money profit, but at the team's *profit-making efficiency*, so we need to move on to a second calculation, which starts with the Gross Profit in £ that we have just looked at.

If you divide the team's Gross Profit (in £) by one of the figures we started with, namely the team's billings (also in £), and you then multiply the answer by 100, you arrive at the team's Gross *Margin*, which is expressed not in £ but as a percentage.

The Gross Margin % shows you *what percentage of a team's billings exceeds the salaries* that have been paid to generate those billings. If you have a highly-paid team that doesn't bill a lot, common sense tells you that not much of their billing exceeds their salaries, so it'll have a low Gross Margin %. If you have a team that bills way more than its lawyers are paid, so that a lot of its billings are in excess of their salaries, a high Gross Margin % reflects that. Teams of lawyers should thus simply strive to build a high Gross Margin %, where as much of their billing is left over after the team's lawyers have been paid to do that billing.

And what should a team's Gross Margin percentage be? Generally and simply – and again – higher! That really is the answer. Whatever the Gross Margin is at the moment, the Team Leader's role and the team's lawyers' role is to influence – in the right direction – the main thing that can make the Gross Margin go up. That is, get team billings up so that team billings exceed the team salary bill by more and more.

Having said that, a team's Gross Margin "just needs to be higher", I can give you some numbers that can help you to understand what particular Gross Margins mean:

- If a team bills less than its salaries, it won't have a Gross Margin at all, as *none* of its billings exceed the team's salaries. Gross Margin – 0%

- If a team bills slightly more than its salary bill (say £1,100 of bills against a salary bill of say £1,000), that is a bit of a gross profit but not much – a (low) Gross Margin of 9%. Absent big billing later, or a compelling reason to offer this work-type, there is little point having this team – all it's doing is paying its own salaries.

- If that same team bills *double* its salary bill (i.e., billings of £2,000), then it follows that *half* of its billing is profit for the firm – a Gross Margin of 50%. That's better. That means that after team salaries have been paid, the other £1,000 goes "into the pot", and the business can use it to pay the central overheads like rent, Business Support salaries, insurance, and so on. But it still doesn't leave any real profit after that, as all the money has been used up.

- If that same team can grow its billing so that it bills £3,000 against the salary bill of £1,000, then that is a Gross Margin now of 66%. Now we're talking! It means that not only are the team's salaries covered, and not only are the firm's overheads covered, but there is also a real profit left over for the owners, pay rises, bonuses, investment in the business, etc.

From these numbers, you can see where you need to be driving your team's Gross Margin.

"But what if one team's Gross Margin is a lot higher than another team's?" I'm often asked. That's always going to be the case. It's not a comparison you should ever make – it's irrelevant. This isn't a competition between teams in a firm. We are all on the same side. We need to ascertain a team's Gross Margin not so we can compare one team to another. Rather, we use the figure so that we can compare a team this month to the same team last month, and so we can push that team to make an improvement next month.

The strongest and best-performing team in The Perfect Legal Business model is not just the team with the highest Gross Margin. It is also the team whose Gross Margin improves month after month after month. *An ability on the part of lawyers to change is precious!*

In a nutshell, the Team Leader's main role in The Perfect Legal Business is to drive the team's billings up and its debtors down. That is done by all the ways we look at in this book – having only Perfect Lawyers in the team, Pride in Pricing, defining retainers, good Utilisation by the lawyers (chargeable hours), good Realisation levels by the lawyers (no write-offs), adhering to the Service Pledge, and having the right team structures in place so that file storage and time-snatching is avoided. It is all achieved, in essence, by a team of lawyers performing as Perfect Lawyers.

And, of course, profit is something that exists only on paper until bills are paid. The Team Leader's job is forever to be the cash policeman, too, though where the lawyers in the team all have a "Cash Commitment", this is not the task it may once have been.

I suspect that if the Team Leader kept the "crown jewel", that is the team's Gross Margin, to themselves, it would be a bit like pushing a rock up a hill in the dark. Far from keeping it secret, therefore, I advocate that ownership of a team's Gross Margin is passed to the whole team. They can then see it as a measure of their own collective business efficiency, and they will hopefully adopt the team-like behaviours and priorities necessary to get the Gross Margin up – particularly if those behaviours are enshrined in the firm's reward and promotions apparatus. Team Gross Margin – and improving it – is then a matter of team pride!

When a firm goes on a business-improvement journey, a team's Gross Margin can improve in Month #1. That of all teams can. The Perfect Legal Business constantly uses this measure of business efficiency to make sure that it doesn't slip in any team in any quarter, or – if it does – that remedial action is quickly taken by the relevant Team Leader/s and their lawyers.

The Perfect Legal Business, through its individual Perfect Lawyers, therefore works hard to drive profitability on every case and in every team. It and its lawyers also ensure that all profitability is turned into cash.

But if we stopped there, all we'd have is a business that dealt well and profitably with any case that came in. As one case completes, another is needed.

A difference between the Perfect Legal Business and an imperfect one, and between the lawyers in both, is where they look as a priority to find those new cases.

5. EXTEND MAXIMUM CARE TO EVERY CLIENT

Subject, of course, to the work-types it offers, The Perfect Legal Business makes sure it gets all the legal work that every one of its clients has. They don't tolerate their clients using different law firms for different things, not least of all because, out of a sense of caring for the client, they don't want the clients getting inconsistent or mediocre (or worse) service levels from another firm.

Although many lawyers have great relationships with their clients, it is not unusual for the relationship to be a transactional one rather than a "wider-relationship" one. A client usually engages with a lawyer for something defined – to deal with a claim, or to deal with their divorce, to buy a house, to acquire a business, or to deal with a Tribunal case.

The relationship, if there is one, is often between the client and a particular lawyer, rather than between the client and the firm as a whole.

The result of this can be that different lawyers in a team can have their own client banks, and different teams in a firm can have their own client banks. Each bank is owned by a team, or by individual lawyers in the teams.

It is not unusual, following on from this, that a client (particularly a corporate client) might use more than one law firm for their various legal needs.

Firms are often surprised when I ask them to map out the fees they have earned – by work-type – from their Top 100 clients. They can do this with what I call a Client Matrix (also called a Gap Analysis), which might in its simplest form look like this:

Client	Dispute Res Fees	Real Estate fees	Employment fees	Corp fees
A	25,000			
B		14,000		
C				120,000
D	125			
E			19,000	

This is not an unusual situation. It represents one of the easiest opportunities to find profit-rich and cash-rich growth. It beats many of the roads that firms travel down as they seek the growth that they need. Fruit does not hang much lower than this.

What does the above table tell you? It tells me:

- The firm has had a big litigation case on for Client A. What an opportunity to get under the skin of that business and to show how your firm can care for its clients.

- One of the Real Estate Partners who looks after Client B is wittingly or unwittingly keeping the client to themselves.

- The Corporate team had a big deal on for Client C. If it was a sale, the client has probably gone (but were the owners looked after, and did they have all their affairs in order?). If it was a purchase, just imagine how much legal work the enlarged business will have.

- The firm has had one small debt recovery matter from Client D. What a great opportunity to start a relationship with the Finance Director. From small acorns, etc. The Listed corporate client I mentioned in Chapter 5 had given my firm a small Debt Recovery case that no one in the firm wanted to touch. I took it and went to visit the FD…

- The Employment Partner who looks after Client E is wittingly or unwittingly keeping the client to themselves.

All the while, the Employment, Real Estate, Dispute Resolution, and Corporate Teams are having meetings with the Marketing team to look at ways for them to try to win new clients.

The Perfect Legal Business does not focus on winning new .001s. It's hard work, it's expensive, it's uncertain, and it attracts new clients whose first question will often be, "What's your lowest price?"

The Perfect Legal Business instead focuses on making sure that it gets all the legal work that all of its clients have. And it will have a good chance of getting all their work too, because it has nothing but Perfect Lawyers and teams who work together to deliver a very good service – every lawyer, every time. A Perfect Lawyer doing, say, Employment work for a commercial client is not going to come up against much resistance when they invite the client to engage with their Property and Corporate colleagues.

But this colleague-to-colleague internal market won't develop if the culture in a firm works against it. For example, if a colleague in one team simply doesn't trust the work or service levels of a colleague in another team (or of a whole team; it happens), you cannot expect them to involve that colleague (or team) in the clients they have long looked after so well. That's why The Perfect Legal Business has nothing but Perfect Lawyers and a Service Pledge across the firm – so that every lawyer trusts every lawyer.

It also won't work if there's a "staff turnover" issue at the firm. If you have a lawyer with a nice basket of lucrative clients and you cannot be certain that they are going to be staying at the firm, the last thing they're going to do is bring their basket of clients into the centre of the firm. And you won't get it if individual lawyers think *they* own the clients.

Colleague-to-colleague introductions are fine and can be effective, but I have seen that there are never as many of them as you would like there to be. Everyone's too busy. Instead, there has to be *central* ownership of and access to all clients – access that is unfettered by over-protective, territorial lawyers.

If the broad "all round care, for the long term" message is strong, and the clients are brought into the centre of the firm rather than being put in a silo (in that they're brought into the client club that we looked at in Chapter 2) and the service that every lawyer delivers is a great service, then the ground is very fertile for harvesting a wider crop of cases from every client.

This will happen naturally if all the parts of the jigsaw are in place – but there's no harm in moving things on a little. Using the Client Matrix and Gap Analysis can help enormously, directing marketing effort to particular clients in relation to particular work-types. "Out there", it's called Key Account Management. It involves talking with clients.

As part of this, instead of setting up a seminar and then wondering who to invite to it, it can be as easy as identifying 100 existing clients of the firm for whom you don't do Employment work, and setting up a seminar for them.

In this way, events are found for clients, instead of clients having to be found for events.

In saying that the Perfect Legal Business focuses on its existing clients rather than on new clients, that is not to say that there is no "marketing" and that a Marketing team has no role.

Far from it, there is a huge opportunity for effective, meaningful marketing here – it just has a different focus to marketing that is always aimed at potential clients "out there". The Marketing team's role and workload is enhanced, as is the teamwork between them and the lawyers in the firm. No more "us and them".

New cases from new clients (.001s) come at a price and sometimes come without profit. Compare and contrast that to .007s, which come from "repeat" existing clients that you already know as a firm and that have already proved their value to you as paying, value-buying clients.

Instead of celebrating new client acquisitions (the profitability of whose work may be dubious when you take into account the hard bargain they've driven and all the "added value" that they wanted "throwing in"), The Perfect Legal Business has as one of the KPI's that everyone in the firm owns and tracks "Percentage of clients at .007".

What's the point in adding another .001 to a pile of work that is already too high for you to service properly and profitably?

Based on my experience, I am a firm believer in the proposition that .007 is where it's at. As I mentioned earlier, it is indeed a license to bill.

6. EXTEND CARE TO CLIENTS PROACTIVELY

In Chapter 3, we looked at the ability to extend care proactively to clients to help them avoid trauma, delays, and expense, using what I call "platforms".

I believe there is a great opportunity here for law firms to do something life-changing for their clients. But not by *selling* to them. Rather, by *proactively caring* for them.

As I set out in Chapter 3, we did this in my firm with our Portfolios. It works. It is an utterly good thing (and a very profitable thing) for a law firm to do. "Care" and "cash" go hand-in-hand here.

The Perfect Legal Business needs to build ways to educate its clients and design solutions for any clients who face risks.

Not doing this is like a patient visiting a dentist with a sore tooth, and the dentist only looks at the tooth that the patient points to.

As sure as eggs are eggs, something is coming down the track at some time. For all of us and for all clients. Shall we let all our clients carry on gambling? Or shall we help them to save a fortune in time, money, and trauma? Do we actually care about our clients, or just about getting some fees from them?

These "platforms" are many things at the same time – things to be proud of, differentiators in your marketplace, and generators of good fees.

Where the opportunity breaks down here, of course, is where a lawyer takes the view that "*My* clients are *my* clients, and you're not *selling* anything to them". This is wrong in so many ways. That view has no place in the Perfect Legal Business, and it forms no part of the make-up of The Perfect Lawyer.

How can you truly care for a client, and how can a lifetime's care in the broadest sense be extended to a client, if the firm is not "allowed" any engagement with a client other than through, say, one Commercial Property lawyer who looks after a client's leases?

7. HAVE THE RIGHT MANAGEMENT STRUCTURE IN PLACE

I am often asked, "What is the best management structure for a law firm?" I always answer with a musical analogy.

Take, firstly, a jazz band – relaxed, casual, chaotic even, with everyone doing things their way. It can be hard to see who the leader of the band is. There might not even be one.

That may work for a jazz band, but I am absolutely convinced that it is no way to move a firm of solicitors towards being The Perfect Legal Business.

And it is no way to get all the lawyers in a firm to operate as Perfect Lawyers in all the ways discussed in this book.

Lawyers are brilliant people. I know – I am one. That's a strength, but not always. Absent a team focus, absent a set of team-like behaviours in place of a range of personal behaviours, absent a clear set of rules and rails, and absent a commitment to constantly support a fixed and limited number of initiatives in a certain way, what happens? The result can be multiple, unconnected efforts and initiatives (sometimes in silos) that are costly in terms of time and money, and which get shelved when there is no quick success.

The results will also include a failure to adhere to internal policies that are designed to protect the business, and a widescale leaking of the profit and the cash that the business should be making and which it needs to be making.

Now, compare the jazz band to an orchestra. Sat within the ranks of the musicians in an orchestra may be world-class pianists or violinists. Stars, on a global scale, perhaps.

But they all look to the conductor to ensure that they are fully in step with the direction of travel and the speed of travel of the piece they are playing, as they are playing it in a team environment. They do not insist on doing, or even remotely feel able to insist on doing, things their own way.

The conductor's role does nothing to diminish the standing or repute of the violinist. Quite the opposite. The violinist recognises that without that overall guidance (and leadership) from the conductor, they'd be part of a shambles rather than part of an exquisite team. They are all team players, working under a team leader.

This is a far more relevant and effective model for law firms that wish to perform at a high level and to change up a gear.

My clear view is always that there needs to be leadership in a law firm within a defined framework, on the one hand, and a commitment on the part of the lawyers to do what the team and the firm needs – in the way that the firm and the team needs it – on the other.

8. OPERATE AS A TEAM, AND DON'T TOLERATE BEHAVIOURS THAT ARE NOT TEAM-LIKE

If lawyers don't do what is needed, none of this will happen. Lawyers can't want all the good things that will flow for them if a firm performs as a Perfect Legal

Business, and not do things the right way themselves. These prizes come from *everyone's* work, not *everyone else's*.

The firm should not take for granted, though, that everything that it needs will be secured from its lawyers straightaway. Education on and induction into all the ways discussed here are necessary, and not in a "flash in the pan" kind of way.

With law firms, I often set up internal academies or universities, where everyone – absolutely everyone in the firm – goes through the rinse *regularly* to keep everything in sharp focus.

This relates to training in all the "soft" ways discussed here, and all the "harder" legal and compliance training can be brought in, too, so that all training and development is delivered by the same organ in the same way and in the same wrapper.

Talking of "compliance", there needs to be universal acceptance by everyone at the law firm that we operate in a highly regulated environment. It is our licence to practise. It is our quality mark over the various pretenders "out there". It is our licence to earn money and – if you are The Perfect Legal Business – to print money. These regulations are our friend, not our enemy. Lawyers make a good living out of interpreting rules and small print, but can baulk when any apply to them.

Why is compliance with the firm's policies and professional policies seen as optional in many firms? Partners and Team Leaders can often be the worst offenders. So much Management time and so much Business Support team time is spent making up for the fact that lawyers haven't complied with internal and external rules and regulations. Let's get over it and deal with it like professionals.

The Perfect Legal Business secures this compliance with internal and external requirements and regulations by creating an environment where compliance is part of the DNA of the lawyers, by way of the ongoing training mentioned just above at the firm's Academy, but also by rewarding compliance on the one hand and not tolerating non-compliance on the other. It also secures it by ensuring that the Partners in the firm lead by example.

Don't brush non-compliance under the carpet just because someone bills a lot! It'll cost the firm more in the long run.

9. REWARDING THE RIGHT THINGS, AND MAKING PEOPLE GREAT (OR GREATER)

This whole thing is a two-way street. If it wants to be The Perfect Legal Business, the law firm needs to have – indeed *create* – Perfect Lawyers. And to reward them, to keep them as such, and keep them at all.

As part of this, the firm needs to offer its lawyers a visible and transparent career path which sets out – in clear terms – what is required of lawyers at various levels, and what they'll get in return. Great people need somewhere to go – or they will go.

This needs to be not just a career path that is "off-the-shelf", but one where the current priorities of the business are enshrined, pushed, monitored, and rewarded. Lawyers' progression is not treated in a pedestrian fashion but in an active way, with a twice-yearly and meaningful appraisal process that has a promotions and reward round straight after each financial year end. The business should have plans for its people, and it should actively push its people so that they grow in themselves and in their careers.

NOW IT'S TIME TO GO LARGE!

With all of the above aspects in place, and with all lawyers exhibiting "perfect" behaviours, the business is truly a Perfect Legal Business that enables and encourages its lawyers to continue to be "perfect".

It is *now* time to do what law firms often, wrongly, do first. That is, try to grow in the ways I looked at earlier, including by spending a lot of time and effort on marketing to win new clients.

Now, look at the marketing that can be done. It is far more powerful than it ever could have been – you have differentiators that you deliver on.

And there is far more – and more effective – marketing and BD being done because *all* your people can convey a powerful message out there. And they will do it proudly. I recall well one of our secretaries coming to see me on a Monday morning because she had met a business owner over the weekend and she had explained to them that we offered "A great service – every lawyer, every time", and that business owner wanted to talk with us.

Of course, not all people or businesses will be allowed into your firm now, as you have "new client" rules in place, but those that do come in will get a great service and you will make maximum money out of them across your firm, for a long time to come.

CHAPTER 12

PULLING ALL OF THIS TOGETHER

So, Chapter 11 details the nine main areas that The Perfect Legal Business and its Perfect Lawyers focus on, to change clients' lives and to secure the sustainable growth in profit and cash that a legal business needs. Try stopping a law firm that embraces all of these things.

It's all about *people*. The people in a law firm are the beginning, the middle, and the end of everything. The lawyers in a law firm are of fundamental importance. Or rather, their behaviours and attitudes are. Lawyers can change absolutely everything, and quickly. If they choose to, that is.

Having resolved that its people will all be of high quality and positive and team-like in their approach, and having put in place structures that reward and recognise these contributions, The Perfect Legal Business makes sure that it only recruits people of this type and that it also retains all these great people. It will also make them better and better – for themselves and for the business.

It invests time and money in their development. It offers security and all the rewards that a successful business can offer.

All of this adds up to something really quite spectacular – including an enviable Employer Brand. Not only does a strong and positive Employer Brand help a firm to retain talent, and by definition to develop that talent and take it to new heights, but it also acts as a beacon out there in the competitive talent marketplace.

Great people want more than money – they want direction, challenges, involvement, security, opportunities, investment, and to be part of a great and winning team. They want to work with other great people.

All of this is only possible if the firm is *constantly* making good profit and good cash. Such is the financial make-up of a legal business, and such are the financial (cash) pressures, that Management can very quickly be called away from all of this lovely work to focus on counting money in and money out. Then the party's over.

Once the elements discussed in this book are all ingrained in the firm and its lawyers, *then* it is time to really "go large" and to get "out there" and make some real noise. Your external marketing and Business Development will now be so much more meaningful and powerful.

Now it will be time to bring in hopeful new clients, to filter them out, to set out the ground rules, to deliver an amazing service, to look after them proactively, to get all their legal work, and to make maximum profit and cash while you do so.

Without these elements being ingrained, you may be rolling out a flawed model where a ton of effort gets you a pound of return, and where the cash impact of your efforts may be deleterious (in cash terms) rather than beneficial.

If you bring a random set of high-achieving people together into a law firm, with no common vision or direction, no clear values and "rules", and no common understanding of *why* everyone is there, where everyone is allowed to behave as they want (and they have been so allowed for decades), it is inevitable that you arrive at a certain kind of creature. Particularly where people have joined that firm from disparate other firms over the years. You cannot help but have built a firm where there is no conformity.

The results can be silos, with local, departmental loyalties rather than firm-wide loyalties. There might be behaviours that are anything but team-like. And people doing things their way, with all the missed opportunities that go with that.

In such circumstances, any growth of the business might actually make things worse, as the firm brings more and more people of varied make-up, backgrounds, experience, ambitions, agendas, and behaviours into the firm without truly inducting them into a particular way of doing things.

Compare a firm like that to one made up of focused people, all of whom are working to the same plan in the same way.

If the two types of firms were rowing boats of the racing variety, one would be going around in circles because the crew were not working together, and the other would be powering through the water with the whole crew smiling, ready for beers and celebrations together after winning the race.

In The Perfect Legal Business, not only is everyone rowing, but everyone is rowing hard, and each person is rowing hard for each other and in the same direction, for the good of the boat rather than for the good of themselves.

Their boat is unstoppable because it holds *a team* full of what we can call Perfect Lawyers.

The people in a firm need to be and act like one team, not lots of individuals or lots of teams. There has to be zero tolerance – not just by the firm but *by everyone in it*, too – of contrary behaviours.

Without this, the result is not just like a car driving with the handbrake on. The car will also have a poorly-running engine, with no Sat Nav, where everyone is arguing over who gets to sit in the front. It will have plenty of passengers but not enough drivers.

But if we think we can get to be "The Perfect Legal Business" and to be "Perfect Lawyers" easily, we are kidding ourselves.

CHAPTER 13

OBSTACLES

I mentioned in the Introduction to this book that I had had three "dawnings" during the writing of this book, which had helped me to see that "The Perfect Lawyer" cannot be created in, or exist in, a vacuum:

- Dawning #1– You can't actually have Perfect Lawyers without The Perfect Legal Business

- Dawning #2 – You can't have The Perfect Legal Business without Perfect Lawyers

- Dawning #3 – There's an issue we need to face up to. We all know where improvements can be made in a firm, and firms have tried for years to achieve most, if not all, of them. *Why aren't these changes made, and why aren't these improvements achieved?*

Or – to put it another way – let's talk about the herd of elephants in the room.

Every law firm has a starting point. Every law firm is where it is. Unless you're going to argue that always delivering a great service is not something to aspire to, or that making good (and growing) profit and cash in a sustainable way is not vital, or that having and keeping great people in the firm and giving them all a great future is not important, let's push all these aspects in every firm. Let's get some *change* to maximise all of these things.

Unless a law firm is doing very well on *all* the fronts discussed in this book, it follows that there is opportunity (if not a need) for a firm and its lawyers to work together to improve things. That is, for them *to change*.

There is clearly already a desire (or need) for change in many law firms. I see that desire all the time:

- A CEO telling lawyers to bill more.

- A Team Leader telling lawyers to get time-recording up.

- A Finance Director telling lawyers to get their bills paid.

- A Head of Marketing telling lawyers to do more BD.

These are all ways by which a firm tries to achieve the change *it* wants. Law firms and their Management have been using these blunt instruments year after year. They'll be using the same blunt tools next year, and the year after, unless the way they seek change *changes*.

These things don't work on lawyers — and they imply that it's for the lawyers to make all the relevant changes.

Why is "change" so hard in a law firm? You could do it all tomorrow. Change is all too rarely achieved in law firms.

I think there are a number of "*core*" reasons for this, and then a *particular* reason.

Core reasons for the lack of *change* in law firms

- Change is okay, provided it doesn't affect anyone personally.

- Lawyers are simply too busy. It's a game of survival, every day.

- Managing Partners can have caseloads or billing targets that impinge on their ability to drive change.

- Team Leaders who could nurture change "on the ground" have caseloads and personal billing targets that are too high.

- Law firms need cash. That translates through to *billing*. No change (or even temporary interruption) to that as the priority can be countenanced.

- For as long as lawyers' "pay" is related to personal billing, no lawyer is going to switch priorities.

- There isn't enough in the way of direct reward if change is embraced.

- There isn't enough in the way of accountability and sanctions if change is not embraced.

- Change is demanded of people by the firm in a piecemeal way, rather than as part of an exciting, explained "Grand Plan".

- There is often no "champion" in a team or a firm who can galvanise everyone into focused action.

In addition, there is, I believe, another overriding reason why most of the time, things don't move forward as they might.

Yes, I am referring to *meetings*.

Meetings

Meetings are a mainstay of law firms. But a root cause of the inability to make progress in implementing any changes – having sat through thousands of them in my time – is how *meetings* can go in law firms. They can be hard work.

I think that the reasons for this include the following (and I was guilty of many of the things I say here during my career as a lawyer, while the firm was using blunt instruments and a lot of meetings to try to get myself and my colleagues to change):

- Big decisions are obviously made at senior "Partners" meetings, where it just takes one Partner who wants to keep doing things their way for the wheels to come off.

- Arriving at *any* decision can be hard. Arriving at lots of good and joined-up decisions which are not diluted by being designed by "committee", and which are free of fudges and compromises, in a short space of time, is nigh on impossible.

- By their very nature, lawyers argue about everything – it's what we do!

- Listening to other lawyers is a much underused skill.

- "Giving something a go" doesn't come naturally.

- Senior people in a team or staff meeting can be intimidating, so junior people might not talk.

- One senior lawyer can derail a meeting – 'seen it many times'.

- There is a lack of self-awareness; for example, around the propensity to argue about everything and not be decisive.

- Lawyers (Partners in particular) are entitled to a say, and they always want a say.

- It's hard in a meeting to say "No" to someone – particularly someone senior – so the firm might progress things that weren't in the original plan.

- Other lawyers can sit in meetings nodding and saying nothing; they've already decided how they're going to do things (that is, the same way as before).

- Even if a lawyer wants to change, a few manic hours or days back in the line of fire makes workarounds very attractive.

- Meetings to discuss changes and plans are unfocused and lose direction. Meetings last hours. Nothing comes of them. People come to dread meetings rather than see them as booster sessions.

Even when something new *is* tried, keeping all the cats herded and moving in the new direction gets harder *within days*. Rome wasn't built in a day – we need to stick with things – not throw them on the fire as soon as there isn't an amazing success.

The chance of making so many decisions and making all the right ones at the same time – and then putting all those decisions into effect across multiple lawyers and teams for the long term – is almost asking the impossible.

Change has to come by everyone actively embracing something new. But you don't get a bird to fly to a new perch by shouting at it; you have to put some seed on the new perch. So, whether it's at Partner meetings to get the big initial decisions made, or meetings of all of your people where you are trying to get them to shape and embrace the new things, the first things needed are:

- An individual and a collective acceptance that some things can improve. Look at the areas I have worked through in this book, and list those where you think you need to do better.

- An open cataloguing of elephants in the room.

- An overall picture of what success looks like in key areas.

- An explicit understanding of what is needed from each person in the whole team to achieve each area of change.

- A framework delivered by the business which shows people it is safe to let go of "the old".

- And having given everyone the courage to let go of "the old", the business needs to give them good reason to actively reach out for "the new".

Yes, all it takes is a decision by each lawyer that – with immediate effect – they are personally going to change. But that will be greatly assisted by the business ensuring that everyone knows what and why, and that everyone knows that such change will be recognised and rewarded.

And as law firm Partners regularly say to me, "Making a decision here is one thing. Implementing it is another thing altogether".

A handful of clear, understandable decisions is a lot easier for a law firm to implement than a large basket of vague, unconnected, fudged plans that no one has been involved in or believes in.

If you're doing it on your own, once you've made some decisions and are in the throes of implementing them, share the good news with all your people as things progress – and share the bad news. Just share the news!

Of course, everything is a trial. If it doesn't work after a big effort for a reasonable time, then change it. But give it a good go!

One way to get a head start and to really make progress is to get an outsider in to facilitate and catalyse things – that's what they're skilled at. Businesses "out there" think nothing of doing that. One law firm Managing Partner I was talking with, however, actually said to me, "I like the sound of it all, Simon, but if I got you in it would be seen as a sign of weakness on my part".

I can't think of a bigger sign of strength than getting a specialist in, and there are plenty of them around. I wish I'd done it when I was Managing Partner. It's what I do with firms now, and the decisions (which are all good and all joined-up) that can be made in days are astonishing. And I never allow a meeting to last more than an hour. People aren't robots. They have feelings.

Businesses out there think nothing of getting external expertise in. It's all the more valuable in law firms, as everyone in a law firm is doing their day job at 100 mph. An external expert brings fast focus and keeps you focused. They don't walk on eggshells. There are no sacred cows. They ask the dumb questions.

As we've seen, there are things needed from lawyers on the one hand, and from the law firm on the other. But there's a vital collaboration that needs to take place *between* a law firm and its lawyers if a law firm is going to get over all the challenges to growth that I listed in Chapter 7:

- The firm and the lawyers need to recognise that they are both on the same side.

- The lawyers need to constantly ask what they need to do and how the business needs them to do it.

- Having been told, they need to apply their skill, energy, and brilliance to *actually* change the way they do things.

- The business needs to deliver to its people, in return.

- The firm has to reward not just high performance, but also the ability on the part of a lawyer *to change*. An ability to change is – to my mind – one of life's great skills, and having been a business-owner and a law-firm owner, an ability to change was one of the greatest and most uplifting attributes I saw in a lawyer. If they could change, then there was no limit to where they could go.

Having been a Managing Partner of a large law firm that needed to make a lot of changes and having seen dozens of other law firms "up close and personal" that would benefit from change, I think the simple sayings are the best. Like, "If you want different results, why are you still doing things the same old way?"

- "The Perfect Legal Business" and "Perfect Lawyers" don't just appear out of nowhere. For there to be improvement, a firm needs to *change*, and its lawyers need to *change*.

- *Crucially, firms need to change the way they pursue change.* Are you still trying to secure change by doing things the same old way – those long meetings, sending round emails, etc?

The need for change is not just in the directions discussed in this book. We live in an era of change – ongoing change. Change is here to stay.

If you want everything to stay the same, a lot has to change.

As well as being good at law, be good at *change* – it's a superb business advantage. Get ahead, whilst all your competitors are sat in those long meetings.

Examine why you might not be good at change. It's probably because of the factors I listed above. Learn to get over these obstacles. Be a business that "does" – and even enjoys – change.

The outcomes of changing – in the ways described in this book – are a "win" for everyone… the clients, the business, and everyone in it.

Surely not even the most brilliant lawyer can think of arguments against that?

Simon McCrum, 2025

Other Books from Simon McCrum

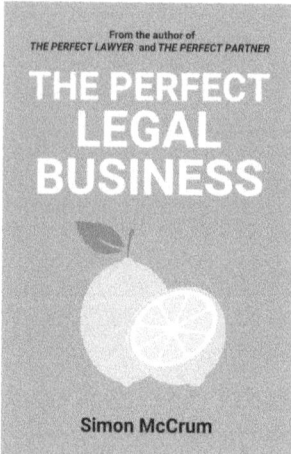

The Perfect Legal Business

What if a law firm's sustained success isn't about billing more and more hours, but shaping its structure, approach, and attitude differently?

In *The Perfect Legal Business*, Simon unlocks a fresh framework for the modern legal firm, built around a number of key pillars including: intelligent client selection, proactive client care, purposeful senior and middle management, higher pricing for a higher level of service, lawyer inputs (not outputs), and the importance of cash to the business – all brought together into a powerful force by the glue that is leadership.

This book invites you to dig deep into law firm management as a constant and fluid problem-solving enterprise – one driven by lawyers at all levels – that seeks to change the fortunes and destinies of law firms, their owners, their people, and their clients.

Note: *The Perfect Legal Business* is the sister book to *The Perfect Lawyer* in that it looks at many of the same themes, but from the viewpoint of the business. As such, it contains material that crosses both titles. As you already have a copy of *The Perfect Lawyer*, you won't need *The Perfect Legal Business*.

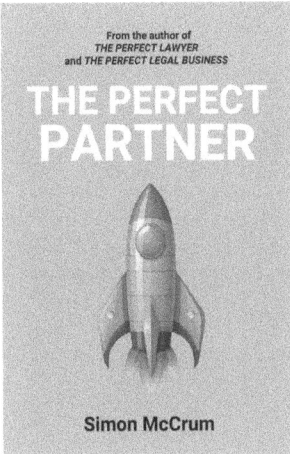

The Perfect Partner

If you've made it to Partner, or you're determined to become one, what are the key qualities and strengths required of a Partner in a modern-day law firm?

In *The Perfect Partner*, Simon examines what makes a Perfect Partner from the viewpoint of numerous key stakeholders, including clients, colleagues, and the business itself. Detailing the characteristics and behaviours that a Partner needs, the book digs deep into a Partner's commercial contribution to the business, their relationships with staff and other Partners, business development, accountability, compliance, and much more. And all under the central umbrella of making a profit and growing a business.

Working through the layers of value (or destruction) that a Partner can bring, Simon arrives at a surprising conclusion. Measurable things count, but other more human things *count more*. If that law firm rocket is going to take off, and prove able to shoot for the stars, each Partner – and all the Partners together – need to focus unequivocally on a 'magic ingredient' to make the firm unstoppable.

Have you got what it takes to be a Perfect Partner? And, just as importantly, have your Partners got the right stuff, too?

www.ingramcontent.com/pod-product-compliance
Lightning Source LLC
Chambersburg PA
CBHW041145230326
41599CB00039BA/7175